5. Producing your portfolio of evidence 26

What you need to do 26

Assessment 26

Separate or integrated portfolios? 27

Evidence Tracker for IT Level 3 28

Planning your portfolio 29

Example portfolio 30

How the example portfolio covers the evidence required 52

6. The external assessment 53

Exam technique 53

The Exemplar Test 54

How did you do? 58

7. Answers 59

Planning and selecting information 59

Developing information 60

Presenting information 60

Taking your skills further 61

Exemplar Test – model answer 64

Appendices 68

A   Information Technology Level 3 – Unit Specification 69

B   Action Plans – including a completed version 73

C   Witness Testimonies – including a completed version 75

D   Proxy Qualifications 77

E   Where to find out more 79

F   Glossary 80

This guide is not specific to any particular software packages. There is, however, an assumption that you have access to the following types of package:

★ Word-processing package

★ Database package

★ Spreadsheet package

★ DTP package

An introduction to Key Skills

1

1

Key Skills are...

Generic skills that help to improve learning and performance in:

★ Education and training   ★ Work and life in general

They are important in:

★ learning   ★ career and   ★ personal life

Key Skills aim to...

Develop and recognise skills in:

- obtaining and interpreting different types of information
- using, developing and communicating information to meet the purpose of studies, work and other activities
- effectively presenting results

Curriculum 2000

From September 2000, if you are a Curriculum 2000 student, you will be aiming to achieve Key Skills units alongside your main programme of study. Just like any other subject, Key Skills need to be taught and developed before you can produce succesful final evidence.

Key Skills will play an important part in widening your studies and experiences along with other initiatives, such as community service or any other 'enhancement' studies. You could also consider any full-time or part-time employment you have which could give you the opportunity to develop and evidence some of your skills.

You will be using many of the skills already without even realising it. Take a look at Appendix D (pages 77–78) where you will see the list of qualifications that you may already have and that could give you exemption(s) from some parts of the Key Skills Awards. (Make sure you ask your teachers for an up-to-date list. This one was current in June 2000.)

From 2000 onwards, many students will also use the opportunities presented by their Citizenship studies to develop and evidence their Key Skills. Every qualification you study from September 2000 will be sign-posted for its opportunities for Key Skills development and evidence.

Letts

EDUCATIONAL

**KEY SKILLS
LEVEL 3**

Survival Guide

Key

Skills

Level 3

Information Technology

Author

Sue Dent

Contents

1. An introduction to Key Skills 4

    Curriculum 2000 4

    HE, Key Skills and the world of work 5

    The individual Key Skills 5

    Key Skills levels 6

    Where will my Key Skills evidence come from? 6

    How are Key Skills assessed? 7

    The Key Skills Qualification 7

    Considering the wider Key Skills 8

2. What you need to know – IT Level 3 9

    Getting started 9

3. Where are you now? 11

    Self-Assessment Test 12

    How to score your Self-Assessment Test 14

    What your score should tell you 14

    How to develop your IT Key Skills 15

4. What the specifications mean 16

    Planning and selecting information 16

    Developing information 18

    Presenting information 21

    Taking your skills further 24

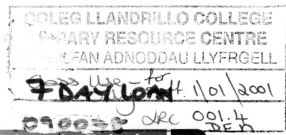

HE, Key Skills and the world of work

- Higher Education institutions are working on developing the Key Skills of their students in order to make them more autonomous and effective learners.

- The points that will be awarded by UCAS for applicants for HE in September 2002 for each of the Key Skills (Communication, Application of Number and IT) will be as follows:

Level	UCAS points per unit
Level 4	30 points
Level 3	20 points
Level 2	10 points

(To see the specifications for Level 2 and Level 4 you can visit the QCA website on www.qca.org.uk)

- Key Skills will also form an integral part of the curriculum for the new Foundation Degrees which will be launched in September 2001. These degrees will be designed to build on the breadth of study and Key Skills that you gain from Curriculum 2000.

- Employers have always loved Key Skills. They may not have called them that, but they constantly ask for people who can work both in a team and on their own. They want people who can quickly synthesise information and present it in an appropriate form. They like employees who are accurate with numbers and can use IT to enhance the content and presentation of their work.

'Key Skills are skills that are commonly needed for success in a range of activities in education and training, work and life in general. The Key Skills units aim to develop and recognise candidates' ability to apply these skills in ways that are appropriate to different contexts in order to improve the quality of learning and performance. They are intended for everyone, from pupils in school to chief executives in large companies.'
Guidance on the Key Skills Units, QCA (2000)

The individual Key Skills

From September 2000, new Key Skills will be launched. There are six Key Skills:

- **Communication (C)**
- **Information Technology (IT)**
- **Application of Number (N)**
- **Working with Others (WO)**
- **Improving own Learning and Performance (LP)**
- **Problem Solving (PS)**

- The first three are often known as the 'hard' or main Key Skills and the last three as the 'soft' or 'wider' Key Skills. This book will concentrate, along with the other two volumes in this series, on developing your 'hard' Key Skills. These are the three that will attract UCAS points.

- Each Key Skill has separate units up to and including Level 4. All the units for each level are presented in the same way. Level 5 is assessed by way of one single integrated unit.

Key Skills levels

Level 1	A student working at this level might be in the first year of a GCSE course or might achieve a D-G at GCSE.
Level 2	A student who is capable and able to gain A*-C at GCSE should be working at this level.
Level 3	Students working towards A/S, A Level and GNVQ/Vocational A Levels should be capable of this level in some or all of the Key Skills.
Level 4	Students working at undergraduate level should be developing skills at this level in some or all Key Skills.
Level 5	This is a managerial, postgraduate level and is gained by putting together a large body of evidence to demonstrate application of these high level skills. Note: generally you would need to be in a role/job that would allow you to demonstrate competence at this level, i.e. managerial or supervisory.

Not everyone will be at the same level in every Key Skill or wish to progress to the same level. You may feel that you will not need to achieve Level 3 in Application of Number to follow your career goal or you may find that IT at Level 2 is sufficient at the moment. Key Skills awards allow you to achieve at the level most appropriate for **you**, while giving you the chance to develop. It is always possible to pick up your Key Skills at a later stage and develop them further. **You should also bear in mind that some students will have chosen subject combinations at post-16 that give them more opportunities for Key Skills developments than others.**

It doesn't matter which awarding/examining body your school or college uses, as all the requirements for achieving your Key Skills are identical. Institutions may use the same awarding body, which will accredit your other qualifications, or they may choose one awarding body to accredit all their Key Skills candidates.

Where will my Key Skills evidence come from?

Your teachers and tutors will be working to make Key Skills attainments as straightforward as possible for you. A great deal of your evidence for the individual units will come from work that you undertake for your other subjects. You will also find that one piece of work can cover the requirements of more than one Key Skill, for example one essay may cover elements of Communication, IT, Working with Others and Problem Solving. It is important that you get to grips with the Unit Specifications – if you understand them well you can plan to get the maximum Key Skills material from each piece of work. In this way you will be gaining extra qualifications without giving yourself a great deal of extra work.

How are Key Skills assessed?

There are two elements to the assessment of Key Skills.

1. A **portfolio** of naturally occurring evidence which will be:
- **internally assessed** (by your tutors/teachers)
- **internally verified/moderated** (teachers check each others' marks to make sure they are all working to the same standards)
- **externally moderated** (by a representative from the awarding body to assure that all internal marking is to the standard required)

2. An **external assessment instrument** to assess:
- **knowledge/understanding**
- **externally set tasks**

You have to pass both of these elements in order to achieve your Key Skills unit(s). The Unit Specifications tell you everything you need to know in order to do this.

The Key Skills Qualification

Every Key Skill is available in its own right as a free-standing unit. But those students who achieve the **three** Key Skills – **Application of Number, Communication and Information Technology** – will receive a national certificate of units **and** the Key Skills Qualification.

It doesn't matter at what level you get the Key Skills, as they will be profiled, for example two at Level 3 and one at Level 2.

The Key Skills Qualification is a profile of achievement in three Key Skills units:

> **Portfolio and Test =**
> **COMMUNICATION**
> **+**
> **Portfolio and Test =**
> **APPLICATION OF NUMBER**
> **+**
> **Portfolio and Test =**
> **INFORMATION TECHNOLOGY**

Considering the wider Key Skills

The specifications for the three 'wider' Key Skills – **Working With Others (WO)**, **Improving Own Learning and Performance (LP)** and **Problem Solving (PS)** – are important to the worlds of study and employment, and for your personal development.

Your school or college may or may not enter students for the wider Key Skills: this does not mean that you should ignore them. Even if you are not aiming for a formal qualification in the wider Key Skills, you will find that you will benefit personally and academically if you aim to develop these skills and gain unit certification.

Working With Others (WO)

In school, college or in part-time employment, are there situations where you have to:

- agree objectives, who does what, when and how?
- organise your time and tasks in order to achieve what you have agreed?
- work co-operatively with others (even if you don't like them!)?
- review what you are doing and consider whether better ways of working can be devised?

Improving Own Learning and Performance (LP)

In school, college or part-time employment, are there situations where you have to:

- identify and agree targets and action plans yourself to meet these targets?
- follow your action plan and gain support and feedback from others when necessary to enable you to meet your targets?
- realistically review and assess your progress and provide evidence of this progress and your achievements?

Problem Solving (PS)

In school, college or part-time employment, do you ever have to:

- identify, consider and describe problems?
- identify and compare different ways in which you could solve problems?
- plan and put into place a solution?
- devise, agree and apply methods for checking that a problem has been solved and review approaches to tackling problems?

If you can say 'Yes' to any of these, have a close look at the Unit Specifications for the wider Key Skills at Level 3. You probably already have the potential to produce evidence that meets the specifications.

(For more details on the wider Key Skills, visit the QCA website at www.qca.org.uk)

These are the outlines of the requirements for each level of IT:

Level 1	Level 2	Level 3	Level 4
Candidates must be able to: • find, enter, explore and develop relevant information • present information, including text, images and numbers, using appropriate layouts, and save information	Candidates must be able to: • identify suitable sources, carry out effective searches and select relevant information • bring together, explore and develop information and derive new information • present combined information, including text, images and numbers, in a consistent way	Candidates must be able to plan and carry through a SUBSTANTIAL activity that requires them to: • plan and use different sources and appropriate techniques to search for and select information based on judgements of relevance and quality • use automated routines to enter and bring together information, and create and use appropriate methods to explore, develop and exchange information • develop the structure and content of their presentation using others' views to guide their requirements, and information from different sources	Candidates must be able to produce at least one EXTENDED example that requires them to: • develop a strategy for using IT skills over an extended period of time • monitor progress and adapt their strategy, as necessary, to achieve the quality of outcomes required in work involving the use of IT for TWO different COMPLEX purposes • evaluate their overall strategy and present outcomes from their work using a presentation showing integration of text, images and numbers

It may be useful for you to look at Levels 1 and 2 for IT, as there is an expectation that if you can achieve Level 3 you can do everything required in Levels 1 and 2. Your teachers/tutors may be able to help but, if not, try having a look on the QCA (Qualifications and Curriculum Authority) website – the address is www.qca.org.uk

Getting started

All the units for each Key Skill at every level, up to Level 4, are presented in the same way.

Each Key Skill unit has a **Unit Specification**, which is divided into three parts:

PART A	A description of what the candidate needs to know
PART B	An outline of what candidates must do
PART C	Brief guidance on activities and examples of evidence

(If you haven't already seen a Key Skills specification, you will find the full specification for Information Technology Level 3 printed in Appendix A on pages 69–72.)

The first things you need to do are **read** the Unit Specification and **understand** what is required of you.

The Unit Specification tells you clearly what the unit is about. IT Level 3 is about **applying your IT skills to suit different purposes**.

You must demonstrate through your portfolio that you understand when it is useful to use IT in your work and that you use it appropriately.

REMEMBER...

None of your IT work should be stand-alone exercises – it must clearly be set in context. That is why you need to plan.

In **Part A**, there are three main headings covering:

Planning and selecting information

Developing information

Presenting information

Part A prescribes the skills that you will need to have or develop to be successful at Level 3 IT.

Below is a breakdown of the skills/techniques required to achieve Levels 1 and 2 in Key Skills IT.

If any of these seem vague to you or you do not understand what the terms mean, then get some help. At Level 3 it is assumed that you can already do all of the things in Levels 1 and 2.

LEVEL 1 IT You need to know how to:	For example:
Find different types of information	Text, images and numbers from IT sources (files, CD-ROMs) and non IT sources (notes, lists, diagrams)
Decide what information is relevant for your purpose	In order to help you answer questions, solve problems or write an essay
Enter and bring in information using formats that help development	Copy and paste text, import clip art images and use features such as consistent use of spacing, tabs and returns, formatting of numbers, line thickness and shading
Explore information	Asking questions of your information, trying things out and seeking alternatives
Develop information in the form of text, images and numbers	Organising information, carrying out calculations
Use appropriate layouts for presenting information, including text, images and numbers	Selecting screen displays for different types of documents, e.g. memos, reports, letters
Present information in a consistent way	Fonts, bullets and number lists, alignments, size and position of images, tables of numbers
Develop the presentation to meet your purpose	Organising your document by moving, deleting, inserting and copying information
Make sure your work is accurate and clear	Check content is relevant, proof read and use spell-check; ask others for their comments; select and highlight information to improve its clarity
Save information so that it can be easily found	Use suitable folders/directories and filenames to make it easy to identify and find your work

LEVEL 2 IT You need to know how to:	For example:
Identify suitable sources of information	Hand-written sources, files on disk, the Internet, CD-ROMs, databases etc.
Search for information using multiple criteria	Operators, such as 'and', <, >, and search engines.
Interpret information and decide what is relevant	To answer an essay question, produce coursework, solve a problem
Enter and bring together information using formats that help development	Using copy and paste, importing images, text and numbers; using tabs to align text; using tables or frames to position information
Explore information as needed for your purpose	Follow lines of enquiry; make and test predictions
Develop information in the form of text, images and numbers	Link information, organise under headings, generate charts and graphs from data, select records or fields and prepare reports from a database
Derive new information	Compare information from different sources to reach a conclusion, use formulae to calculate totals, averages etc.
Select and use appropriate layouts for presenting combined information	Margins, columns, headings, borders for images and texts, tables, spreadsheets
Present information in a consistent way	Use of paragraphs, layout, font sizes, size and style of images and text
Develop the presentation to suit your purpose and types of information, including text, images and numbers	Highlight information to improve its impact; refine layouts; make sure that it suits your purpose and audience
Ensure your work is accurate and clear and is saved appropriately	Proof read, spell-check and seek the views of others; use suitable folders/directories and file names; how to avoid losing work

Self-Assessment Test

The Self-Assessment Test on page 13 is to start you thinking about Key Skills and give you a feel for what Level 3 IT is about.

Now, be honest with yourself and go through the self-assessment, ticking the most appropriate boxes. See page 14 for how to score the test.

YES You can always do this and have lots of evidence that you could use to demonstrate/prove your skills.

MAYBE You do some of this but as yet you are not very confident that you **always** do it.

NO This is something you do not feel comfortable with and you need opportunities to learn and practise.

click
click

The questions are not framed in the language of the Unit Specification but are a range of general statements that can be used as an aid to start you thinking about your use of IT.

SKILL	Yes	Maybe	No	SCORE
1. PLANNING AND SELECTING INFORMATION				
Can you plan a substantial activity by breaking it down into a series of tasks?				
Can you compare the advantages of different sources of information – databases, files on disk, CD-ROMs?				
Do you choose appropriate techniques for finding information – database query techniques, Internet search engines?				
Do you make selections based on relevance to your purpose and judgements on quality?				
2. DEVELOPING INFORMATION				
Do you enter and bring together information in a consistent form (lists, tables, types of images) and use automated routines, macros, icons, report routines?				
Can you create and use structures and procedures for developing text, images and numbers?				
Can you sort and group information, mail merge, generate graphs, analyse and interpret statistical information using a spreadsheet?				
Do you explore information, design and develop lines of enquiry, test hypotheses?				
Can you derive new information from your evaluation of information from different sources and can you justify your conclusions?				
Can you use methods of exchanging information to support your purpose – email, shared access to documents, collaborative development of information?				
3. PRESENTING INFORMATION				
Can you develop the structure of your presentation, changing paragraph style and automatic referencing?				
Do you use the views of others to help you, obtaining feedback on layout, content and style?				
Do you develop and refine the presentation of text, images and numbers to improve the impact of your work?				
Do you present information so that it meets your purpose and the needs of your audience, comparing paper-based, single form etc. and choose the most suitable?				
Do you always ensure that your work is accurate and makes sense, proof reading, using the spell-check and asking the advice of others?				
TOTAL				

How to score your Self-Assessment Test

Score as follows:

2 marks for every 'YES' you ticked

1 mark for every 'MAYBE' you ticked

0 marks if you ticked 'NO'

What your score should tell you

This assessment is just a quick way of showing you where your strengths and weaknesses lie. YOU CANNOT FAIL THIS ASSESSMENT!

If you scored:

30 or 0   You are far too optimistic or too pessimistic. Do the assessment again!

14 +   This is a more realistic result. What this would suggest is that you already have many strengths to build on but you need practice in a range of skills in order to get to the right level. This book offers opportunities for practice and offers suggestions for further improvement. You should be able to achieve Level 3 with careful planning. You might even consider Level 4.

Below 14 If you think that you have answered accurately, then you need to think very carefully about how you are going to develop those areas where you are weak. The exercises in this book will help but it might also be useful to investigate what support and help you can access at school or college. It may well be that you have always felt that you lack confidence in some areas and it is now a good time to get to grips with this before going to HE. Try to get the skills for Levels 1 and 2 in place. This will give you more confidence and then have a look at the assessment again.

If you use IT fairly regularly you should be at Level 1 or 2 at present. However, many students do use IT but do not have the specialist vocabulary to support their skills and do not always use the most appropriate software package for their purpose. We will be helping you with these issues in the rest of this book. Using IT accurately and appropriately can be an enormous support for all of your other studies and your future career – that is why it is included in the Key Skills.

So remember, this assessment gives some idea of your **attainment** but does not assess your **potential**, which, as far as this book is concerned, is much more important. This is exactly the same principle that your teachers use in selecting you for A/S, A Level or Vocational A Level study. They know how you performed in GCSEs and they assess that you have the potential to achieve your higher level qualifications. The main point is that you now have some idea of what you can do and know, and what you need to do and know. **You** have the job of bridging this gap.

DIAGNOSTIC TESTING   Many schools and colleges have diagnostic tests, which you can sit to identify your existing level of Key Skills and to identify those skills that need development and practice. You should ask your tutors for advice.

How to develop your IT Key Skills

The great thing about Key Skills is that they are rather like those Russian dolls that fit into each other: the lower levels all build to the higher levels. If you develop and practise the skills for Level 1 and then Level 2 you can 'add' the extra skills needed for Level 3 as you develop them.

Go back to the Self-Assessment Test and remind yourself which skills you need to acquire and develop.

All of the qualifications you are taking will be clearly signposted with opportunities for generating Key Skills evidence.

The intention of Curriculum 2000 is to offer you a broad base for your studies while developing a range of skills to help you progress to higher level study and the world of employment. You should consider your other qualifications carefully, with the help of your tutors if necessary, and identify where the Key Skills occur in these qualifications. This is the **ideal** way to approach Key Skills, by generating evidence within your wider studies. **Integration** will make Key Skills more relevant and manageable.

PROXY QUALIFICATIONS

Some qualifications, which you may already have achieved or be working towards, give exemption from parts of some Key Skills. There is a list of these in Appendix D (pages 77–78). (This was accurate as of June 2000.)

If you think you are entitled to any exemptions, get your tutor to check for you.

KEY POINT

They are **your** Key Skills and as a Level 3 candidate the awarding bodies consider that **you should be very active in developing your skills**. You are not a passive recipient of knowledge. You should also apply this to your learning strategies for your other subjects.

As you read through this section, you need to refer to the Unit Specification for IT Level 3 (see Appendix A on pages 69–72).

Planning and selecting information

REFER TO THE UNIT SPECIFICATION AS YOU READ THROUGH THIS SECTION

The importance of planning

- Planning is essential if you are to produce a portfolio and external assessment of the calibre required for Level 3 in IT.
- You must then 'select' (weed out) the material that is not appropriate.
- IT Level 3 requires you to think about the purpose of the work you are producing.
- You will be assessed on your ability to make judgements about suitability for purpose.

Where might you already use these skills?

- Do you use them at school/college or in your part-time employment?
- You already plan when you are required to produce essays, presentations, reports etc. in other subjects.
- If you use a database at work, for example with customer records, you may also be using IT skills. Do you do any stock ordering or send out any letters?

Quality of information

- The information that is available via the Internet is often very up-to-date. Keep this in mind when using statistics etc.
- Unfortunately, the information on the net is not always of a high quality and you should always question why it is there.
- When searching for data, you should be familiar with techniques for more advanced search features, such as relational operators (less than, greater than) and logical criteria (AND, OR, NOT).
- Important – your assessor will expect to see IT skills demonstrated in a very planned and structured way in your portfolio work, through at least **one** substantial activity that includes tasks for 3.1, 3.2 and 3.3.

The substantial activity you use could be drawn from other subjects that you are studying **but** you may have to go a little bit further with this work to fully demonstrate your IT skills. Here is an example.

An investigation into degree courses in your chosen subject

Use Internet to research UCAS	IT 3.1
Scan materials in prospectuses	IT 3.1
Produce table of degree courses and show no. of places on offer and likely UCAS offer Compare with your predicted grades	IT 3.2
Use this hypothesis to identify likely courses for you	IT 3.2
Produce a presentation for your tutor group using OHTs and handouts to explain your findings Get feedback from group	IT 3.3
Write a report on your findings, including images, a table and graphs/charts (minimum three sides of A4)	IT 3.3

This table is a suggestion of how an activity could be planned using a topic that you may already be investigating. Obviously, it is only the outline of an idea but you might like to think along these lines when planning your own work.

Compare the advantages and limitations of different sources of information

- Most educational institutions have some Internet access and the majority of them have CD-ROM based materials. There is a wealth of newspapers that are now archived to CD-ROM, making it easy to backtrack on articles etc. for research.
- Although you must demonstrate that you can research computer-based resources, the requirements of the specification do not say that you only have to use computer-based sources. Remember this when considering how you can make a comparison of sources and their advantages and disadvantages.

Choose appropriate techniques for finding information

- You need to be comfortable with a range of techniques for finding information, in particular information that fits a specific criterion or range of criteria. Think about key words and phrases when performing searches.

TIP

Finding and using information is a skill that transfers across all of the key skills. You must always be aware of the opportunities you have to develop and demonstrate this skill.

- You will need to demonstrate that you can use relational operators (<, >) and logical criteria (AND, OR, NOT).

Make selections based on relevance to your purpose and judgements on quality

- Make sure that the presentation **and** the content are appropriate for the purpose and audience.
- Use the skills here that you have developed in your English GCSE and in any Communications Key Skills sessions to aid your judgements.

By getting to know the Unit Specifications for all of your Key Skills you can start to make connections. Pieces of work that you use for evidence in one Key Skill may also cover some of the evidence requirements of another Key Skill.

Evidence you create for the section above may also cover:

Communication		3.2
LP	3.1	3.2
N	3.1	

★ See page 8 for further information on the wider Key Skills.
Visit www.qca.org.uk for detailed Unit Specifications.

EXERCISE

1. Using the **Internet**, list at least three search engines.

2. Find and list two sites that would give you information about genetically modified foods.

3. Using a **CD-ROM** for *The Guardian*, find and print out two articles concerning GM foods.

4. Using email, either:
   - send a letter to a friend telling them what you have found out about GM foods and print out from the screen, or
   - send an email to one of the sites in **2** above, requesting more information. Print out from your screen.

See Chapter 7 for example answers.

Developing information

REFER TO THE UNIT SPECIFACTION AS YOU READ THROUGH THIS SECTION

- You will need to be able to produce a document(s) that is consistent in style, demonstrating automated routines.

- Many students at A/S and A Level are dealing with concepts that concern 'models' and hypotheses. You could test these using IT.

- Most subjects offer opportunities for statistical prediction. You could develop a spreadsheet to incorporate multiple and linked calculations (use of relative and absolute referencing, IF/THEN conditions, lookup tables).

- Always back up your work and keep copies so that the chances of losing it are minimised.

- Be prepared to justify your conclusions and to show your methods.

- Don't forget to develop your skills for sharing information, such as email and shared access to documents. Engage in collaborative development of information with other students.

- **Annotating** your work is very important in Key Skills. You moderator(s) will wish to see the process of your developing work. You can move paragraphs around, use different fonts, change the page orientation from landscape to portrait etc. When you have done this, write on your printouts and identify the changes you have made and say why you made them.

Enter and bring together evidence in a consistent form

- Show that you can change font styles and sizes and that you can embolden and italicise your work.

- If you import from one document into another, make sure that the typeface and size follow through. Don't leave it looking like a cut-and-paste job.

- You need to demonstrate your use of automated routines. You could set up a macro to put a personalised header or footer on your documents.

- You must customise both applications and appropriate routines.

Create and use structure and procedures for developing text, images and numbers

- IT Key Skills specifications at **all** levels require you to use all three elements of text, number (this means using numbers, not just typing them in) and images.

- If you have collected data in a spreadsheet, can you produce a bar chart or a graph and label it correctly?

- Can you use templates and paragraph styles and restructure or recreate them?

- It might also be appropriate to get a Witness Testimony from your tutor to confirm what you are doing in terms of using a variety of techniques. Don't forget any changes to your Action Plan that might arise from your work in progress.

- While a Witness Testimony should not be the only evidence for an evidence component, it may, if appropriate, be used as supporting evidence.

Explore information

- This can be demonstrated most easily with numerical data and, if you plan at the beginning of your portfolio, you will make sure that the information you gather gives you ample opportunity to demonstrate the skill of exploring information.

- The Vocational A Level (VCE) in Travel and Tourism would give students plenty of opportunities to undertake investigations into their subject area and produce good Key Skills evidence. The specification for the VCE suggests how this can be planned into the programme. For example, in the compulsory Unit 1, Investigating Travel and Tourism, a student could begin developing IT evidence by undertaking the following project. (In Chapter 5 this is developed into portfolio evidence.).

> **A project to plan a group end of term outing to Alton Towers**
>
> You are going by coach and need to plan the costings, including entry, meals and coach fare. Your friends have identified the maximum they would be prepared to pay for the day.
>
> 1. Work out the cost per student if the whole group travels.
> 2. You could try altering the date/time in order to see what impact that has on costs.
> 3. Get different quotes from coach companies.
> 4. Set up a 'break even' investigation to ascertain the minimum numbers needed to run the trip.
> 5. Present information to a) tutor group and b) course tutor.

Derive new information

- If you have planned and developed your information with a clear focus, new information should follow, often as the solution to or conclusion of your task.

- Show how you have synthesised the information from different sources. Use formulae and logical relationships to 'explain' numerical data.

Use methods of exchanging information to support your purpose

● Email is perhaps the most straightforward way to provide evidence of this skill. You could email organisations for information.

● You could consider corresponding electronically with students in other schools or other countries to jointly develop project ideas. Keep printouts of these 'conversations' or other evidence that they have taken place.

● Be prepared to be honest about your contribution to the whole. Don't claim work that you have not done when collaborating in the development of information.

● If you are contacting companies or organisations, make a note of their website address and email address for any bibliographies you may need to produce.

MAKING CONNECTIONS

By getting to know the Unit Specifications for all of your Key Skills you can start to make connections. Pieces of work that you use for evidence in one Key Skill may also cover some of the evidence requirements of another Key Skill.

Evidence you create for the section above may also cover:

LP		3.2	3.3
PS	3.1	3.2	3.3
N		3.2	
WO		3.2	

★ See page 8 for further information on the wider Key Skills. Visit www.qca.org.uk for detailed Unit Specifications.

EXERCISE

1. Create a **bar chart** from the information in the table below.

2. Label the axes.

3. Ensure that the chart has a legend.

4. Give the chart the title 'Freedom Holidays, Bookings Totals for 1996-1998'.

	1996	1997	1998
Skiing	450	504	663
Lakes	270	324	359
Sun and Sand	1256	1542	1765
Safari	76	98	105

See Chapter 7 for example answers.

Presenting information

REFER TO THE UNIT SPECIFICATION AS YOU READ THROUGH THIS SECTION

- All Key Skills specifications at all levels require you to present your work to a high standard. The specification will guide you.
- Page numbers, footnotes, paragraphing etc. all help to guide the reader through a document.
- Only accurate work will meet the specifications.
- Do not rely on the spell-check to pick up typographical errors, omissions or grammatical errors. Practise proof reading your documents. SPELLING, PUNCTUATION and GRAMMAR are important. Errors seem to be even more obvious when a text is word-processed.

REMEMBER...

Your work in the External Assessment Test and the Portfolio will be assessed on your ability to use spelling, punctuation and grammar to a very high degree of accuracy.

You will be expected to understand and comply with:

★ Copyright – you must not take other people's work or ideas and pass them off as your own. This is at best plagiarism and at worst theft. When using information from any source, be very careful to acknowledge where it came from and, if necessary, get permission to use it. Ask your teachers if you are unsure.

★ Data protection – the amount of information of a personal or sensitive nature that is held on computer is increasing. There are data protection laws to ensure the security of this information and you must conform to these. Confidentiality is crucial, for example in computerised patient records in doctors' surgeries or hospitals, in the courts of law and in banking. Many systems require the use of elaborate passwords in order to protect data. This area also covers such things as backing up data to ensure work is not lost due to theft or a power surge etc.

★ Health and safety risks – there are risks when using computer equipment, for example the glare from the VDU or repetitive strain injury (RSI). There are also the normal risks when using electrical equipment, for example trailing cables and leads, and the requirement not to bring food or drinks into the computer room.

★ Dealing with errors – this is an important skill. You need to be able to diagnose simple faults (Have you turned the power on? etc.) and remedy them, and identify when the fault or error is beyond your control and know who to ask for help.

REMEMBER...

Many or all of these issues will arise during the time that you are producing your Key Skills evidence. You may refer to some of them in your portfolio or your tutor/assessor may observe or question you on them so that you can demonstrate your knowledge. You may also be questioned on these aspects of IT in the external assessment.

Error log

From the time you start developing your Key Skills IT, you should keep an error log. Keep it in your folder of work and jot down whenever you encounter any problems. You need one column for the problems and another column next to it where you can write down how you solved the problem. For example:

Error Log	Solution
18/10/00 Printer not working	Rang technician who sorted it.
26/10/00 Network down so couldn't do work	Had to wait for technicians. Lesson cancelled.
4/11/00 Trouble printing grid-lines	Spoke to Mrs Barker who showed me what to do.

Develop the structure of your presentation

- If you are comfortable and competent with the skills in the above sections you should have no trouble with the evidence requirements in this section.
- You should be using routines like pagination and using automated referencing facilities, such as footers with files names and dates etc. Can you modify structures such as templates and paragraph styles?
- You now need to show your work to your friends or your tutors and take into account any comments they make about the presentation of your document. How will you evidence this?

Develop and refine the presentation of text, images and numbers

- All formal documents, such as letters, memos and reports, tend to have a font size no larger than 12 point. You should also be very careful about the style of font you use. Many organisations have a 'house style'.
- If a document is formal, stick to Times New Roman or maybe Arial or Univers.
- Some of the more 'fancy' typefaces detract from the content of your work and might suggest to the assessor that you cannot differentiate between appropriate styles. Leave these for more creative work, such as desktop published documents, posters, flyers etc.
- Numbers are often best presented in tables, so make sure you have an opportunity to include some in your work. You may create spreadsheets or databases and include these in your work. You can use underlining and highlighting techniques to add emphasis where necessary.
- If you can include a DTP document in your portfolio, this is where you can 'go to town' using a range of techniques with word art, borders, overlays etc.

Present information so that it meets your purpose and the needs of your audience

- The Unit Specification requires you to say **why** you have used IT for a particular task or piece of work. Be critical of your methods and somewhere in your action planning or annotation you need to address this issue.

Ensure work is accurate and makes sense

- Proof read, check spellings and let someone else read through your work.
- At Level 3, spelling, punctuation and grammar are expected to be highly accurate with only one or two errors. If you are using a spell-check, don't rely on it to pick up every error. You must check your work through yourself.

By getting to know the Unit Specifications for all of your Key Skills you can start to make connections. Pieces of work that you use for evidence in one Key Skill may also cover some of the evidence requirements of another Key Skill.

Evidence you create for the section above may also cover:

C   3.3

N   3.3

★ See page 8 for further information on the wider Key Skills.
Visit www.qca.org.uk for detailed Unit Specifications.

EXERCISE

Following the Travel and Tourism theme, imagine that you are a student on a work placement as part of your studies.

1. Write a memo to your boss outlining the results for the company, Freedom Holidays, over the years 1996-1998.

2. Import the chart you created in the previous practice task into your document.

3. Print a copy of your work.

See Chapter 7 for example answers.

Taking your skills further

Have a go at the following IT tasks and see how you do. They will give you practice in developing and presenting information at the standard required for Level 3 IT.

You and your friends have been running a stationery shop in school/college to raise funds for a local animal charity.

You must put down your income and expenditure clearly so that your 'books' can be audited. You need to design a way of doing this on your computer.

Task 1

1. Open a suitable application and insert the data from the box below.

RSPCA SHOP	Accounts	Jan - Feb 00		
ITEM	Purchased	Wholesale Price	Sold	Retail Price
Pencils	200	£0.03	100	£0.06
Plastic Wallets	1000	£0.10	357	£0.15
Biros Blue	1000	£0.08	86	£0.25
Biros Black	1000	£0.08	58	£0.25
Rubbers	1000	£0.04	45	£0.15
Wallet Folders	250	£0.15	113	£0.30
Correction fluid	60	£0.42	37	£0.65
Labels	30	£0.56	30	£0.74

2. Improve the way the table looks by using **THREE** formatting techniques to make the title and headings stand out (bold, italic, underlining, changing font size/ style etc.).

3. Use the Auto Sum to total the columns **Purchased** and **Sold**. **Print** out a copy and **save**.

4. Insert a column headed **Wholesale Expenditure** after the Wholesale Price column.

5. Insert a column headed **Retail Income** after the Retail Price column.

6. In the Wholesale Expenditure column, insert a **formula** to calculate the expenditure. Replicate this formula down the column and **Auto Sum** the total.

7. In the Retail Income column insert a **formula** to calculate the income. Replicate this formula down the column and Auto Sum the total.

8. Add a footer, including your name, the date and the task number.

9. Print out your work, making sure it fits on one side of A4 and includes the **grid-lines**.

10. Print out again, this time showing the formulae. Make sure it fits on one page. You may need to change the **Page Setup**.

11. Save with an appropriate name.

Task 2

Your are now going to evaluate your sales performance and consider which items you should or should not stock in future.

1. Add a final column to your sheet and head it **EVALUATION**.

2. In the **EVALUATION** column use an IF formula that will use the cell reference necessary to display:

    a) the word **STOCK** if the sales were 50% or more of the total items purchased.

    b) the word **CANCEL** if the sales were less than 50% of the total items purchased.

3. Update the footer to read **Evaluation**.

4. **Save** with a new filename to show the content.

5. **Proof read** your work and **print** out, showing the calculated values, grid-lines and making your sheet fit one page.

6. Print out again as above but showing your **formulae**.

Task 3

1. **Create** a document for your friends on the fundraising committee.

2. The document needs a **footer** to include the title **Accounts** and the page number.

3. Include an appropriate **Image** at the top of your page.

4. Include a short piece of **text** to explain the findings of your spreadsheet.

5. **Import** your spreadsheet into your document.

6. **Proof read** and **print** out a copy of your work.

7. **Save** with an appropriate filename.

> Have a look at the example answers in Chapter 7. Are your answers more or less identical, excepting Task 3 where you will use your own ideas in your document?
>
> If you can do all three tasks, you should have no problems with the end test for IT. You have the skills necessary for Level 3 work – you must now apply them.

> The skills required for IT Level 3 are extensive and overarching them all is the expectation that you will be critical of your approach and will constantly revise and review what you are doing in the light of your progress. You need to be providing proof of this in planning your evidence and through the annotations you make to your work. An Action Plan can help you with this as a useful checklist for your progress.

Producing your portfolio of evidence

5 | **5**

What you need to do

This section is concerned with the production of your portfolio. For some this will be a new concept, while others of you may have done work in the past that required you to produce portfolio evidence. Don't be fooled into thinking that this is simply a 'project' where you have to put together work in a folder – the expectation is for rigorous standards to be met and it must be approached with that in mind.

The requirements for your portfolio of evidence are laid down in Part B of the Unit Specification (see page 71) and the following points should be kept in mind:

- The evidence referencing must be as laid out in the specification and all work clearly identified as to what reference you are claiming it against.

- The specification requires a SUBSTANTIAL piece of work, which should cover all of the evidence components. At Level 3 it is inappropriate to use bits of work to cover each separate element.

'A substantial activity might be concerned with a survey of transport services, the development of a technical design or the analysis of local business opportunities. Information may be obtained from a variety of sources, including the Internet, practical survey or experimental work.'
Guidance on the Key Skills Units QCA (2000)

- Careful planning of the work to be included in the portfolio is essential.

- Action Plan your work and keep a copy of this in your portfolio showing achievements and any rescheduling.

> On page 28 you will find a blank pro forma Evidence Tracker, which you should start to fill in as soon as possible. You will need to make extra copies, as you will find that throughout your studies you will have many opportunities to develop your Key Skills in IT and you may choose to change the pieces of work you are putting in your portfolio of evidence.

Assessment

Putting together the portfolio can be easy as long as you plan what you will include and then check that you **are** going to cover all the evidence requirements. If not, consider extending your activity/task to cover the skills/techniques that are missing. You can do this using an Action Plan and the Evidence Tracker, both included in this book.

Only when your work is assessed as being of the correct standard will it be put forward for external moderation. You are only required to produce **one substantial** task. If you are sure that this meets the specification requirements, then your portfolio will pass.

Separate or integrated portfolios?

Your Key Skills evidence will ideally come from the other subjects you are studying. This makes the qualification easy to manage and reduces your workload. The question is where will you keep this evidence?

The Key Skills moderator will look at your work to see if it meets the requirements of the Key Skills specification. He/she will not judge it, for example, as a piece of biology or science work. He/she is there solely to judge your Key Skills competence, a separate qualification. A lot will depend on how your school/college organises Key Skills.

You have two options:

1 Keep your evidence in the same place as your work for your other qualifications, for example with your English work, but keep a tracking sheet which clearly outlines for the moderator where the evidence can be found. You and your tutors must make sure that this work is accessible for the moderator.

2 Take a copy of your work, which is your evidence from your other subject, and create a separate Key Skills portfolio.

In both cases the work you are putting forward as evidence will be the same. It is really a matter of which options best suit your situation.

REMEMBER...

All of your work must be original and unaided. The examples in this book are to help you get started. You will be able to find examples of activities that you are already undertaking in your other qualifications or in your enhancement studies that will allow you to demonstrate your own IT skills in a unique way.

Evidence Tracker for IT Level 3

As you begin to gather your evidence you can fill in your tracker sheet, making sure that you cover everything required.

Evidence component	Evidence description	Location	Date
IT 3.1 Plan and use different sources to search for and select information required for **TWO** different purposes. Purpose 1: Purpose 2:			
IT 3.2 Explore, develop and exchange information and derive new information to meet **TWO** different purposes. Purpose 1: Purpose 2: (As 3.1 above)			
IT 3.3 Present information from different sources for **TWO** different purposes (3.1 and 3.2) and **audiences.** Document 1: Document 2: Your work must include **ONE** example of text, **ONE** example of images and **ONE** example of numbers. Text ☐ Images ☐ Numbers ☐			

All of the above should be carefully planned through **one substantial** task.

Planning your portfolio

How you plan to gather your evidence will depend on how Key Skills is set up in your school or college. Are you aiming to get your evidence through the other qualifications that you are studying or are you producing Key Skills evidence in other sessions?

- It is important to remember that you can demonstrate your ability in Key Skills in a wide variety of settings. Indeed the 'transferability' of Key Skills is one of their selling points.

- You must decide what you produce for your Key Skills evidence and how you do it, but if you decide to use work from other qualifications it can mean less work for you.

- There is no doubt that bland subjects tend to lead to bland evidence. Wherever possible, students should use material that they can get their teeth into. A subject that encourages a lot of argument or debate will generally give you lots of material to use, will be easier to research and will give you the opportunity to display your tact and sensitivity.

- Remember: You must **not** come up with any new system of indicating your evidence. You **must** use the referencing system given in the specification.

The most straightforward way to collect your evidence is to plan your progress through the evidence components. Negotiating and discussing a brief with your teacher and producing your **Action Plan** can be really useful.

- An Action Plan is not a requirement for your evidence in IT Level 3 **but** it can be used as evidence for Improving Own Learning and Performance.

- It is also an excellent way of planning and keeping yourself on schedule. You will find an example of a blank Action Plan and a completed version in Appendix B (see page 73).

- You can also use an Evidence Tracker like the one earlier in this section. It will allow you to fill in the components where you have completed work to the specification. It also shows how concise the portfolio should be. Quality, not quantity, is the secret.

Example portfolio

The following portfolio has been created for this book to demonstrate how the requirements of the Unit Specification can be met. The table on page 52 shows how the sample portfolio covers all the evidence required. Previously in this book we have looked at the theme of Travel and Tourism. The evidence in the portfolio might also have been generated by a Geography or Maths student undertaking investigations as part of their coursework.

Comments These comments have been included throughout the example portfolio to highlight how the candidate is meeting the specification requirements.

SARAH FRY
Newtown College

Key Skills Information Technology

Level 3 – Evidence Portfolio

February 2001

Sarah Fry – Key Skills IT Level 3 portfolio

As part of my studies for UNIT 1 in my VCE in Travel and Tourism I have been looking at the impact of tourism on the economy.

I thought it would be a really good idea to get my tutor group to visit Alton Towers, one of the most popular theme parks, and ask the staff and visitors some questions.

I have been discussing with two of my friends such questions as how far people will travel for a day out and how much they are willing to spend. We also want to know how long people will queue for rides etc.

I need to do the following things:

1. Get information on costs for Alton Towers.
2. Get information from friends and families of our group.
3. Report on findings.

IT is really useful for these things and I think people are happier to answer questionnaires if they look professional. It looks as if you know what you are doing and is better than scrappy bits of paper.

IT can also assist me in the calculations I need to do in order to work out the costs for the trip to Alton Towers.

By using IT I can start my work and add to it or change it as I go along.

Candidate explains her rationale for using IT, which is useful for anyone reading the portfolio.

Key Skills Action Plan

The candidate has listed the tasks she had undertaken and when she completed them.

Tasks are linked to evidence.

Where possible links are made with her other Key Skills.

NAME: Sarah Fry

DATE: September 2000

KEY SKILL: IT

LEVEL: 3

DATE	Planned Tasks	Review Date	Completed Date	Evidence Component	Check links with other Key Skills
11/9	Investigate Alton Towers website for opening and prices etc	13/9	11/9	3.1	
12/9	Get names of coaches locally from Yell	14/9	12/9	3.1	
15/9	Design questionnaire for tutorial groups on Alton Towers and preferences	21/9	18/9	3.1/3.2	WWO 3.1
	Design questionnaire to distribute to friends and families	21/9	19/9	3.1/3.2	
7/11	Collate data from questionnaire and produce a table and pie chart	18/11	25/11	3.1/3.2	
	I was delayed because I did not get all the questionnaires back				
5/12	Produce table and pie chart and review progress with Mr Phillips	5/12	5/12	3.2/3.3	LP 3.1/3.2/3.3
10/12	Use mail merge to send letters to coach companies to find out prices	12/12	11/12	3.2	
18/12	Start to design a poster for Alton Towers trip using Publisher including text and images	7/1	5/1	3.3	
10/1	Speak to Mr Phillips about my report on the feasibility and costs of the Alton Towers trip	10/1	10/1	3.3	LP 3.1/3.2/3.3
24/1	Produce report on costings etc, including tables, charts and images, and the findings of the Friends and Families questionnaire	15/2	10/2	3.3	C 3.3

Student Signature S Fry

Tutor Signature R Phillips

Date 15 Feb 2001

Both candidate and tutor sign the Action Plan to confirm the accuracy of this document.

Evidence Tracker for IT Level 3

Student: Sarah Fry

Date: September 2000

> Candidate clearly lists all evidence in her portfolio and says where it is located.

Evidence component	Evidence description	Location	Date
IT 3.1 Plan and use different sources to search for and select information required for **TWO** different purposes. Purpose 1: Cost group trip to Alton Towers Purpose 2: Investigate popularity of theme parks for T + T Unit 1	Action Plan Printout from Internet Examples of questionnaires produced for 1 + 2	This work is in my red Key Skills IT folder	10/11
IT 3.2 Explore, develop and exchange information and derive new information to meet **TWO** different purposes. Purpose 1: Cost group trip to Alton Towers Purpose 2: Investigate popularity of theme parks for T + T Unit 1	Purpose 1 – Table of results collated from returned questionnaires Projections of income and expenditure Copies of letters to coach operators Email to Nicky Purpose 2 –	This work is in my red Key Skills IT folder	18/12
IT 3.3 Present information from different sources for **TWO** different purposes (3.1 and 3.2) and **audiences.** Document 1: Poster for students and report for tutor Document 2: Report for T + T coursework Your work must include **ONE** example of text, **ONE** example of images and **ONE** example of numbers. Text ☑ Images ☑ Numbers ☑	Purpose 1 – Flyer/poster for notice boards to advertise trip Includes text and images Report to Mr Phillips on this trip and my progress so far Includes text, number and images Error Log Purpose 2 –	This work is in my red Key Skills IT folder	15/2

> The candidate shows clearly what she has included as evidence in her portfolio so far and what elements she is claiming it against. As yet, she is only part way through her course and still has to complete her investigation into theme parks. When she has completed this, she should have covered all of the evidence required. It still has to be assessed and moderated.

Official Alton Towers Website

SARAH FRY

I.T. 3.1

SALES

CONTACT US INFO SEARCH

TICKET OFFICE

OFF PEAK PRICES SAVE UPTO £5   Click here to Book

WHEN TO VISIT

PARK

HOTEL

EVENTS

TICKETS

OTHER INFORMATION

Ticket Booth

Terms and Conditions

TICKET OFFERS

Tickets from £16.00 for Adults plus special Advance Booking Bonuses

Alton Towers is open everyday from 1st April to 29th October from 9.30am, rides open from 10.00am. Rides close between 5pm and 7pm and the park closes 1 hour after rides close. (Excluding special events)

This year Alton Towers is introducing "**Lower Price Days**" to give you even better value. If you book in advance you get **FAST TRACK ENTRY** giving you priority entrance at the monorailand allowing you to go straight through the turnstiles to begin your day even quicker. Also check out our other **ADVANCE BOOKING BONUSES** guaranteed to give you an even better day out.

LOWER PRICE DAYS

Save up to 25% during a third of our season. Please note that these are selected days only, please check the calendar

Prices on these days are:

		Prices on selected days from 1st July 2000 to 29th october 2000
Adults		£16.00
Child	❓	£13.00
Family	❓	£58.00

In addition if you book now you can take advantage of the following

ADVANCE BOOKING BONUSES

Get an **XRT** - e**X**clusive **r**ide **t**ime on Oblivion and Nemesis for 1/2 hour before the park officially opens, AND a reserved seat at the 4pm **Barney Show** for no additional cost. Plus don't forget that **FAST TRACK ENTRY** is also included.

SPECIAL DISCOUNTS

On all full price days you can choose to take advantage of our discounts for booking in advance OR pay the full price and take advantage of the advance-booking bonuses listed above. (XRT and Barney)

Prices on these days are:

		Discounted Advance booking price from 1st July to 29th October	Price including Advance-booking bonus from 1st July to 29th October
Adult		£19.00	£21.00
Child	❓	£15.00	£17.00
Family	❓	£61.00	£65.00

Click through to our calendar now and make your choice and book your ticket

Pick Date

http://www.alton-towers..../view.asp?Section=infoSubSection=Events&page=events.ht

**Newtown College
Year 11 Tutorial Groups**

SARAH FRY
I.T. 3.1

Proposed Trip to Alton Towers

Questionnaire

Candidate has created this questionnaire to obtain further information.

Please circle your answers

1. Would you be interested in a trip to Alton Towers in June of next year, 2001?

Yes   No

2. What time of the week would you prefer?

Weekdays   Weekend

3. What is the maximum cost you would pay for the trip?

£5-£10   £11-£15   £16-£20   £21+

4. Would you like the opportunity to save for the trip on a weekly basis?

Yes   No

5. Would you be prepared to help with the organisation, collecting in money etc.?

Yes   No

If 'YES' please fill in your name and form number so that I can contact you.

Please return this questionnaire to Sarah Fry, 11 N.

I have 4-6 more completed questionnaires. This is where the data for my table and pie chart comes from.

Newtown College
Year 11 Tutorial Groups

SARAH FRY
I.T. 3.1

Proposed Trip to Alton Towers

Questionnaire

Candidate annotates work.

Please circle your answers

1. Would you be interested in a trip to Alton Towers in June of next year, 2001?

(Yes)   No

2. What time of the week would you prefer?

(Weekdays)   Weekend

3. What is the maximum cost you would pay for the trip?

£5-£10   £11-£15   (£16-£20)   £21+

4. Would you like the opportunity to save for the trip on a weekly basis?

(Yes)   No

5. Would you be prepared to help with the organisation, collecting in money etc.?

(Yes)   No

If 'YES' please fill in your name and form number so that I can contact you.

Joanne Evans.
11 Z.

Please return this questionnaire to Sarah Fry, 11 N.

Candidate begins to explore information and derive new information.

I had 47 people send back the questionnaire and from their answers I produced a tally chart. I then used this evidence to produce a spreadsheet and pie charts to show the responses in a more visual way. I think it is easier to see the results in a pie chart.

Tally:
N=47

Q1   Would you be interested in a trip to Alton Towers in June of next year, 2001?

45 – Yes
 2 – No

Q2   What time of the week would you prefer?

34 – Weekdays
11 – Weekends

Q3   What is the maximum cost you would pay for the trip?

£5-10   3
£11-15   5
£16-20   34
£21 +   1

Q4   Would you like the opportunity to save for the trip on a weekly basis?

Yes   40
No   5

Q5   Would you be prepared to help with the organisation?

Yes   11

Candidate has clearly laid out results of tally sheet.

NEWTOWN COLLEGE
YEAR 11 – T & T VCE

I am a student in the above group and as part of my Travel and Tourism studies I am looking at the patterns of visiting theme parks. I would be grateful if you would spend a few minutes filling in this questionnaire. The answers will form part of a report for my coursework.

Thank you.

Sarah Fry

1. How many people are there in your household?

   _____

2. Please give the ages of any children. _____

3. Have you visited a theme park in the last 12 months?

   Yes   No

4. If YES – how many times? _____

5. If NO – why not? _____

6. Do you think theme parks represent good value for money?

   Yes   No

7. If NO – why not? _____

8. How far are you prepared to travel to a theme park?

   <50 miles   50–99 miles   more than 100 miles

9. Please comment about the length of the queues for the rides.

   _____

10. Do you find the food and drink good value?

    _____

11. Please give your opinion on the cleanliness of the theme park/s you have visited.

    _____

12. I would be grateful for any comments you would like to make.

    _____

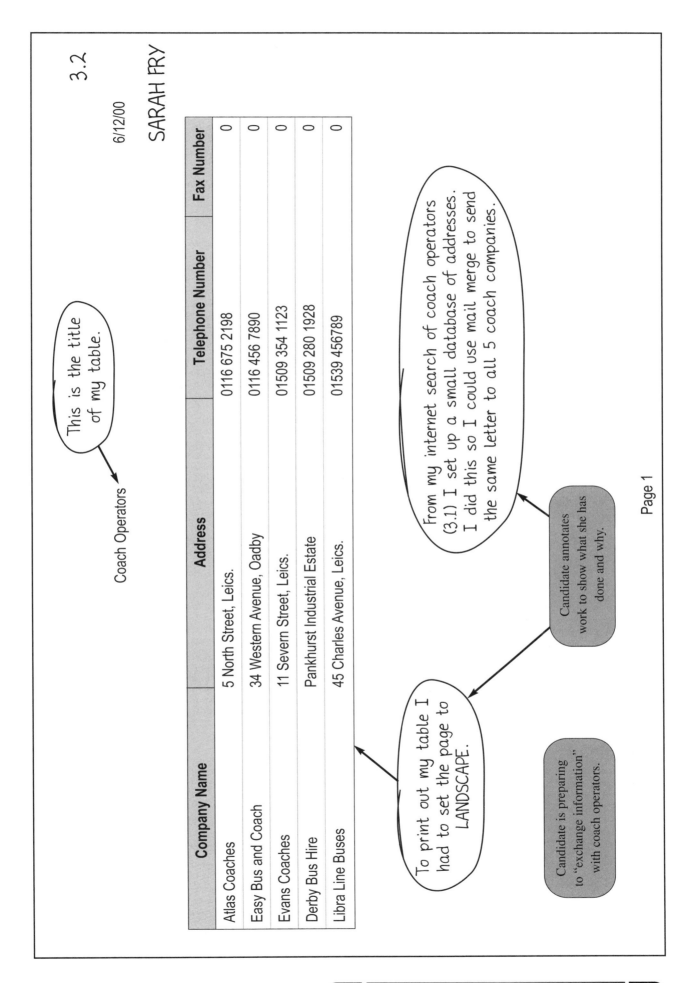

3.2

6/12/00

SARAH FRY

This is the title of my table.

Coach Operators

Company Name	Address	Telephone Number	Fax Number
Atlas Coaches	5 North Street, Leics.	0116 675 2198	0
Easy Bus and Coach	34 Western Avenue, Oadby	0116 456 7890	0
Evans Coaches	11 Severn Street, Leics.	01509 354 1123	0
Derby Bus Hire	Pankhurst Industrial Estate	01509 280 1928	0
Libra Line Buses	45 Charles Avenue, Leics.	01539 456789	0

From my internet search of coach operators (3.1) I set up a small database of addresses. I did this so I could use mail merge to send the same letter to all 5 coach companies.

Candidate annotates work to show what she has done and why.

To print out my table I had to set the page to LANDSCAPE.

Candidate is preparing to "exchange information" with coach operators.

Page 1

Candidate explains the process she has followed.

After creating my database, I produced this letter using WORD. By inserting MERGE FIELDS into the letter I can send the same letter to all the coach operators in my database.

«Company_Name»
«Address»

Sarah Fry
Tutor Group 11N
Newtown College
Main Street
Newtown
Leicester LE7 78Y

11 December 2000

Dear Sir/Madam

RE: Proposed Day Trip to Alton Towers

I am writing to enquire if you would send me details on the hire of the following:

29 June 2001 –

One 45 seater coach from Newtown College to Alton Towers. Returning the same day.

I look forward to receiving your reply.

Sarah Fry

Candidate uses mail merge to facilitate exchange of information with coach operators.

Use of automated routines.

Again candidate shows the changes to her document.

This is how MAIL MERGE inserts the details into my letter.

Atlas Coaches
5 North Street, Leics.

Sarah Fry
Tutor Group 11N
Newtown College
Main Street
Newtown
Leicester LE7 78Y

11 December 2000

Dear Sir/Madam

As these are the main points I put them in BOLD.

RE: Proposed Day Trip to Alton Towers

I am writing to enquire if you would send me details on the hire of the following:

29 June 2001 –

One 45 seater coach from Newtown College to Alton Towers. Returning the same day.

I look forward to receiving your reply.

Sarah Fry

SARAH FRY   3.2

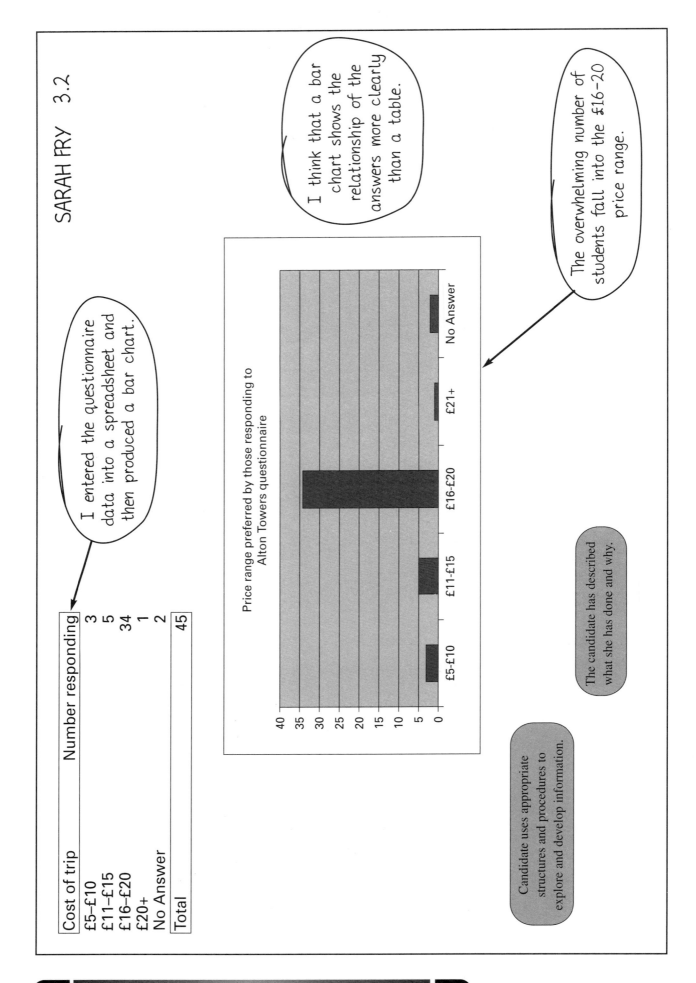

Cost of trip	Number responding
£5–£10	3
£11–£15	5
£16–£20	34
£20+	1
No Answer	2
Total	45

I entered the questionnaire data into a spreadsheet and then produced a bar chart.

I think that a bar chart shows the relationship of the answers more clearly than a table.

The overwhelming number of students fall into the £16–20 price range.

Price range preferred by those responding to
Alton Towers questionnaire

40
35
30
25
20
15
10
5
0

£5–£10   £11–£15   £16–£20   £21+   No Answer

The candidate has described what she has done and why.

Candidate uses appropriate structures and procedures to explore and develop information.

SARAH FRY   3.2

Comparative Costs of Alton Towers Trip

Coach Operator	Price	Cost if 45 Travel	Cost if 35 Travel	Cost of Entry	Total Cost with 45	Within Budget?	Total cost with 35	Within Budget?
Atlas Coaches	£236.00	£5.24	£6.74	£14.50	£19.74	YES ✔	£21.24	NO
Easy Bus and Coach	£198.00	£4.40	£5.66	£14.50	£18.90	YES ✔	£20.16	NO
Evans Coaches	£345.00	£7.67	£9.86	£14.50	£22.17	NO	£24.36	NO
Derby Bus Hire	£276.80	£6.15	£7.91	£14.50	£20.65	NO	£22.41	NO
Libra Line Buses	£238.00	£5.29	£6.80	£14.50	£19.79	YES ✔	£21.30	NO

I used "IF" statements to find this out.

I put the replies from the coach company into a spreadsheet and worked out the costs for 45 students and 35 students. From the results it is clear that we need 45 students to go on the trip to get the price near to £20 per head.

Candidate explores, develops and derives new information.

The candidate has used a range of techniques to interrogate the spreadsheet. She can use formulae.

Comparative Costs of Alton Towers Trip

SARAH FRY   3.2

Coach Operator	Price	Cost if 45 Travel	Cost if 35 Travel	Cost of Entry	Total Cost with 45	Within Budget?	Total cost with 35	Within Budget?
Atlas Coaches	236	=B2/45	=B2/35	14.5	=C2+E2	=IF(F2>20, "NO", "YES")	=D2+E2	=IF(H2>20, "NO", "YES")
Easy Bus and Coach	198	=B3/45	=B3/35	14.5	=C3+E3	=IF(F3>20, "NO", "YES")	=D3+E3	=IF(H3>20, "NO", "YES")
Evans Coaches	345	=B4/45	=B4/35	14.5	=C4+E4	=IF(F4>20, "NO", "YES")	=D4+E4	=IF(H4>20, "NO", "YES")
Derby Bus Hire	276.8	=B5/45	=B5/35	14.5	=C5+E5	=IF(F5>20, "NO", "YES")	=D5+E5	=IF(H5>20, "NO", "YES")
Libra Line Buses	238	=B6/45	=B6/35	14.5	=C6+E6	=IF(F6>20, "NO", "YES")	=D6+E6	=IF(H6>20, "NO", "YES")

The printout shows how I used the spreadsheet to calculate values.

The candidate clearly is competent in using the spreadsheet to help her make decisions.

This was my first poster/flyer. I want to make it more eye-catching.

SARAH FRY   3.3 POSTER VERSION 1.

ADD BORDER ART

Trip to Alton Towers

Change clip art

I showed this to my friends who said it looked a bit boring.

We are taking names for a day trip to Alton Towers for all Year 11 Tutor Groups.

Change some fonts

The trip will be on

June 29, 2001

The approximate cost will be £20 – this includes coach fare and admission.

If you are interested, come to a meeting in the Common Room on

Friday 15 December at 12 noon.

Or contact: Sarah Fry, 11 N

Candidate indicates how she intends to develop her document.

Nicky

From: Nicky <NM@mm2000.freeserve.co.uk>
To: Sarah Fry <SF@mm2000.freeserve.co.uk>
Sent: 9 December 2000 16:25
Subject: Re: Key Skills IT Poster

I think the picture is a bit boring and it doesn't really stand out enough.

If you change those things I think it should be OK.

I'll see you soon.

Nicky

> ---- Original Message ----
> **From:**   Sarah Fry
> **To:**   Nicky <NM@mm2000.freeserve.co.uk>
> **Sent:**   Saturday, 9 December, 2000 3:18 PM
> **Subject:**   Key Skills IT Poster
>
> Nicky
>
> Have a look at the poster which I have designed for the Alton Towers Trip.
>
> Do you think this is OK?
>
> Send me your comments.
>
> Sarah

As it was the weekend I sent Nicky the poster by email. I did not want to wait until Monday and email let me send her the image very quickly. I could have used our fax but Nicky does not have one.

Trip to Alton Towers

We are taking names for a day trip to Alton Towers for all Year 11 Tutor Groups.

The trip will be on

June 29, 2001

The approximate cost will be £20 – this includes coach fare and admission.

If you are interested, come to a meeting in the Common Room on

Friday 15 December at 12 noon.

Or contact: Sarah Fry, 11 N

This document includes text, image and a variety of fonts.

automated routine

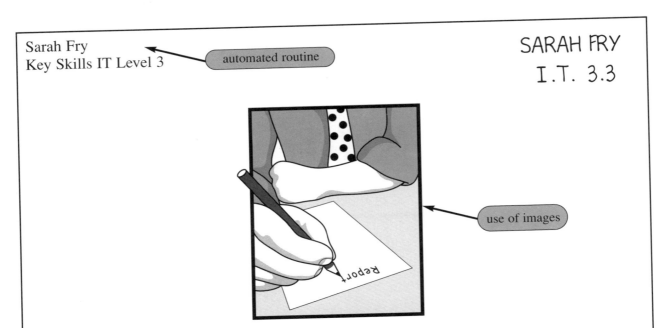

use of images

Report on Investigation into Proposed Trip to Alton Towers to Gather Data for Travel and Tourism Coursework

Background

As a part of my Travel and Tourism course I am looking into the growth of the tourism industry in this country and, in particular, the growth in the number of theme parks. I want to visit Alton Towers, one of the most famous of these, to investigate how far people travel to visit the park and how much they are prepared to spend on each visit.

I have spoken to my T & T tutors about this project and I have told Mr Phillips, my IT tutor, that I will be using a lot of my material as evidence for my IT Key Skill Level 3.

Researching Information

Initially I looked up Alton Towers on the Internet, www.altontowers.com. It was not difficult to find. However, the web pages contain lots of images and take quite a long time to download. The pages are quite exciting and the information they provided was clear. Printouts of the web pages are included in my portfolio.

After searching for Alton Towers, I thought that I would look for addresses for coach companies to find out how much transport was going to cost.

To do this I used www.Yell.com, a search engine that is like the phone book, Yellow Pages. I entered the criteria 'coaches' and 'Leicester' and it produced a list of phone companies for me.

This was useful as I could then get quotes from a few companies to compare prices.

automated routine

1

automated routine

I put the names and addresses of the coach companies into a database and then wrote a letter asking for information. Using the mail merge command I was able to send the same letter to each coach company. If the coach companies had email addresses I could have got the information more quickly. But I still found that using IT to source the information was quick and easy. By using a word processor to write the letters, I was able to produce something that looked well presented and professional.

Company Name	Address	Telephone Number
Atlas Coaches	5 North Street, Leics.	0116 675 2198
Easy Bus and Coach	34 Western Avenue, Oadby	0116 456 7890
Evans Coaches	11 Severn Street, Leics.	01509 354 1123
Derby Bus Hire	Pankhurst Industrial Estate	01509 280 1928
Libra Line Buses	45 Charles Avenue, Leics.	01539 456789

Imported from database. Table = Image

Findings

Lots of people had said that they would be interested in coming to Alton Towers so I designed a questionnaire for all my year tutor groups. Out of 120+, 47 replied. I was able to find out that they would prefer to go on a weekday and that £20 was the maximum price they were prepared to pay.

If I did this again I would ask everyone to put their name on the questionnaire so that I could get back to them with any queries.

When I got the information back from the coach operators I wanted to see what the overall cost per person for the trip would be. I put all of the information into a spreadsheet and worked out the cost if the coach was full, 45 people, and if the coach only had 35 people.

Coach Operator	Price	Cost if 45 Travel	Cost if 35 Travel	Cost of Entry	Total Cost with 45	Within Budget?	Total cost with 35	Within Budget?
Atlas Coaches	£236.00	£5.24	£6.74	£14.50	£19.74	YES	£21.24	NO
Easy Bus and Coach	£198.00	£4.40	£5.66	£14.50	£18.90	YES	£20.16	NO
Evans Coaches	£345.00	£7.67	£9.86	£14.50	£22.17	NO	£24.36	NO
Derby Bus Hire	£276.80	£6.15	£7.91	£14.50	£20.65	NO	£22.41	NO
Libra Line Buses	£238.00	£5.29	£6.80	£14.50	£19.79	YES	£21.30	NO

During the time I was investigating this trip I arranged to speak to Mrs Evans, the College Bursar. She told me that it would be possible to book the coaches etc. through College if my tutor signs the order form. She would then open an account for us and students could go every week to the office and pay some money towards the trip.

Imported from spreadsheet. Use of number.

automated routine ⟶ 2

automated routine

Conclusions/Recommendations

There seems to be enough interest to go ahead with the trip and I am producing posters to put on the notice boards. Nicola Myers and Jane Harrison are going to help me by reminding students in their groups about the trip.

I recommend booking with Easy Bus and Coach Company as they will be the cheapest. We must get 45 people or the trip is not viable, as it would cost more than the £20 that people are willing to pay.

I also recommend that we ask for a £5 non-returnable deposit to make sure that people do not mess us about and change their minds.

I am still waiting for all of my questionnaires from friends and the families of students to be returned. I printed out 150 and they have all been distributed. At present I have about 87. From this information I shall collate the replies and produce charts and graphs. When we go to Alton Towers I will ask a sample of visitors the same questions and make some comparisons. Some of this data will be used for my Application of Number Key Skills evidence.

Sarah Fry
14 February 2001

automated routine

3

ERROR LOG

Student Name : S. Fry

Programme of Study : Key Skills IT – Level 3

DATE	ERROR	SOLUTION
11/9	Couldn't log on to Internet – my password wasn't recognised.	Technician came and sorted it out.
12/9	I couldn't print out because the ink cartridge on the printer ran out.	Saved my work to disk to print out tomorrow.
9/12	Wanted to work on my portfolio but couldn't because the system was down.	No work possible.

How the example portfolio covers the evidence required

IT portfolio requirements for Level 3	Assessment criteria	Portfolio evidence
IT 3.1 Plan and use different sources to search for and select information required for **TWO** different purposes.	• Plan how to obtain and use the information required to meet the purpose of your activity • Choose appropriate sources and techniques for finding information and carry out effective searches • Make selections based on judgements of relevance and quality	Action Plan shows careful planning. Evidence of Internet search. Information on coach operators is selected via use of search engine. Purpose 1: Trip to Alton Towers for students. Purpose 2: Collect data for T & T coursework. *Not yet complete so criteria not met.*
IT 3.2 Explore, develop and exchange information, and derive new information to meet **TWO** different purposes.	• Enter and bring together information in a consistent form, using automated routines where appropriate • Create and use appropriate structures and procedures to explore and develop information and derive new information • Use effective methods of exchanging information to support your purpose	Purpose 1: Information is put into a database from which charts are produced and calculations are made. Using mail merge, information is exchanged with coach operators. Information is also exchanged via email when the candidate seeks her friend's comments on the poster. Automated routines are used. Purpose 2: A questionnaire has been devised to research people's attitudes to theme parks. *As yet the data has not been fully collected or analysed and the assessment criteria therefore are still to be met.*
IT 3.3 Present information from different sources for **TWO** different purposes and **audiences.** Your work must include at least **ONE** example of text, **ONE** example of images and **ONE** example of numbers.	• Develop the structure and content of your presentation using the views of others, where appropriate, to guide refinements • Present information effectively, using a format and style that suits your purpose and audience • Ensure your work is accurate and makes sense	Purpose 1: A poster has been produced after seeking comments from a friend. It is bold and eye-catching and meets its purpose. It is also accurate and includes **text** and an **image.** Purpose 2: As 3.2 above, is still to be completed. *The candidate cannot fulfil criteria 3.3.* When she has collected and collated all her data and presented her findings, including an example of **numbers**, she should fulfil the criteria.

REMEMBER... This portfolio has been created for the purpose of this book. You must produce work that is your own. The requirements of the specification could be fulfilled in fewer pieces of work than this candidate produced, but how you meet the specification is down to your planning and organisation.

TIP Wherever possible, include your assignment brief or write a short rationale for your portfolio. This is not a requirement of the specification but helps the assessor and moderator to appreciate the context of your work.

- Remember that you will not know the 'subject' of the test in the same way as sitting a GCSE in, say, Maths or French but, rather, you will be presented with material upon which you will demonstrate your Key Skills in IT.

- You may be unfamiliar with producing exam answers using computer hardware and software. Practice before hand can help with this.

- You must be comfortable with the language of IT, so you should check in the Glossary (Appendix F, page 80) to make sure that you are producing the correct evidence.

- Obviously you will need access to a PC and a printer in a space that allows you to work without other candidates having a view of your screen. Your teacher(s) should arrange for this and for any technical support to be on standby in case of technical hitches.

- As the new 2000 Key Skills are being phased in, there are only two or three opportunities each year to sit the end test. This should change as the qualification progresses and there is the intention that the end test will be available more or less on demand.

- For the timing of your end tests you will need to speak with your teachers. It may even be possible to send your work down-line to the examiner in future years!

Exam technique

Key Skills external assessments are no different from any other exam or time-constrained assessment. **You must do what you are asked in the time allowed. If you do this, you should pass.**

Although you must be comfortable and confident with **everything** in Part A, you will not be expected to demonstrate **all** of these skills in a $1\frac{1}{2}$ hour external assessment. You will be tested on a sample of skills, for example one external assessment may focus on a spreadsheet while another may require you to produce a database. It is crucial that you prepare thoroughly.

When producing your portfolio you **must** produce evidence that covers **all** of the requirements for Part B of the specification.

REMEMBER...

Do not use an unusual or very large typeface (font) in order to make your work look more than it is – except, of course, to show your ability to change font and size etc. in DTP. Generally, documents should be produced using the default setting, which will be Times New Roman 10 or 12 point. This is what would be expected in a business or academic setting.

At the end of this chapter you will find an example of an IT Level 3 end test. On the front cover it tells you:

WHAT YOU NEED:

- access to a computer, software and a printer – *your school will have arranged this*

- this task book – *will be given to you in the exam room*

ADDITIONAL AIDS

- bilingual dictionaries may be used – *no calculators or other paper-based dictionaries allowed*

TIME ALLOWED – 1 HOUR 30 MINUTES.

To complete this activity successfully you will need to:

- use the information provided in this task book to complete the three tasks
- complete the tasks using the computer and software available – *the type of computer and software are not important. Whether you are using PC-based or Mac-based equipment, you must be certain that you have a range of software at your disposal.*
- give all the printouts appropriate file names – *Tip: don't use your initials for every name – you soon get confused.*

Approaching the questions

The first thing you should do is turn over the paper and quickly scan through the questions – do not write or key in anything at this stage.

The questions

When you turn over the paper you will see that there are three tasks for you to complete. The marks are broken down for you against each element of the tasks.

Task 1	8 elements	21 marks
Task 2	4 elements	12 marks
Task 3	6 elements	17 marks

TIP

Use a pen or pencil to tick off each element as you complete it. It is easy to get lost as you work down the page.

Make sure you have the required number of printouts. Highlight elements where it tells you to print out and you will not get confused.

The source material

- You are provided with all the data needed to produce the database.
- When it comes to Task 3, you are on your own! Spend a minute or two planning what you want to do. Write some notes on your test paper or make a couple of sketches.

The Exemplar Test

Now, find a quiet place with a computer and printer where you will not be disturbed for an hour and a half, and answer the End Test.

When you have finished, go and have a soft drink or a coffee and then you will be ready to come back to check YOUR answers (see Chapter 7).

EXEMPLAR TEST

LEVEL
Key Skills – Level 3

PAPER
Information Technology

THERE ARE THREE TASKS IN THIS PAPER (TOTAL 50 MARKS)

WHAT YOU NEED:

- access to a computer, software and a printer;
- this task booklet.

ADDITIONAL AIDS

- bilingual dictionaries may be used.

TIME ALLOWED – 1 HOUR AND 30 MINUTES.

To complete this activity successfully you will need to:

- use the information supplied in this task booklet to complete the three tasks;

- complete the tasks using the computer and software available;

- give all the printouts appropriate file names.

Instructions to candidates

- Write your personal details in the spaces provided on the cover sheet.

- Do not open this task booklet until you are told to do so by the supervisor.

- Read each question carefully.

- You should attempt all questions.

- Make sure you print out all of your work and that it is clearly labelled.

- At the end of the assessment attach your printouts securely to your cover sheet and hand them along with this task booklet to the supervisor.

Candidates are required to answer all parts of each task. The questions in this paper are all based upon the theme 'Working in a local video shop'.

You work as an assistant in the local video shop. You have been asked to set up a database to enable easy selection of the information stored.

The video shop database will hold details of all the videos which are available for hire. An extract of this information is shown below.

Task 1

1   Create a new database using a suitable file name.   *(2 marks)*

2   Create a table, giving it a title which includes your full name.   *(2 marks)*

3   Create a structure for the table with the field titles shown below. Use appropriate data types for each field.   *(4 marks)*

4   Enter the following details.   *(6 marks)*

Certificate	Video Title	Running Time	Price
12	King Ralph	102	£1.00
15	The Piano	90	£2.00
18	The Shining	120	£1.50
15	Ghost	110	£2.00
15	Back Beat	124	£2.00
18	The Exorcist	105	£2.00
15	My Life	100	£1.00
12	Bird on a Wire	140	£1.00
PG	Free Willy	120	£2.00
PG	Hocus Pocus	95	£1.50
18	Carrie	126	£1.00
PG	Mrs Doubtfire	150	£1.50
15	Sniper	107	£1.00

5   Check for accuracy and print out a copy.   *(1 mark)*

6   Add the details of three videos which have come into the shop for rental. They are all certificate 15, with running times of 105 minutes at price £2.00.

     The videos are Urban Legend, The Haunting and Patch Adams.   *(2 marks)*

7   Sort all the records by certificate in ascending order.   *(2 marks)*

8   Check for accuracy, save your work and print out a copy.   *(2 marks)*

Task 2

1   From the table select those videos which are certificate 12 and cost less than £2.00 to rent.

(4 marks)

2   Arrange the columns so that the video titles appear in the first column and remove the 'Running Time' column.

(4 marks)

3   Use your name in the title for this selection and add the text **'Certificate 12'**.

(2 marks)

4   Check for accuracy, save your work and print out a copy of the selection.

(2 marks)

Task 3

The video shop owner has decided to sell all the videos in the database. You have been asked to produce a leaflet with two printed sides of A4 to publicise the sale. The leaflet must include a list of the videos and a suitable image.

1   On the first page enter a brief statement drawing attention to the sale. Make sure that your font is of appropriate size for a leaflet and is in bold.

(3 marks)

2   Select a suitable image, insert it on the first page and resize it as needed to fit with the text and the page layout.

(3 marks)

3   The second page is for you to show the videos available for sale. Import the complete list of videos, omitting the price field, and place it in a suitable position on the page.

(4 marks)

4   Add a footer with your name, the text **'leaflet'** and with page numbers.

(3 marks)

5   Check your leaflet for accuracy, save it using a suitable filename and print out a copy.

(3 marks)

6   Print out, from the place you saved your work, a copy of all file names you used during the assignment. This can be either in the form of a screen print out or a list of filenames which has been signed and dated by the supervisor.

(1 mark)

END

How did you do?

- In Chapter 7 you will find a model answer. The answer is annotated to show how the requirements of the test have been met.

- You should go carefully through the model answer to check it against your printouts. Is it the same? If not, why not?

- In Tasks 1 and 2 your work should really be identical, apart from font style or sizes you may have chosen. There is little scope for variety here. However, Task 3 is a design task and, as such, you may have a leaflet that looks very different from the example. This is fine as long as you check that you have done everything required.

- Perhaps you felt happy about some of the IT skills needed but less confident about others. Many people use quite a limited range of skills in, for example, word-processing and utilise other types of application less frequently but can easily 'pick up' new skills.

- You would be well advised to get some help with the skills you are less confident with – 'muddling through' leads to bad habits and is not a good way to build IT skills. Many schools and colleges put on support classes for students to develop their IT skills. Often, these are computer-based packages that tutor you at your own pace and at your own level.

- Don't delay in getting help if you think you need it. Developing your IT skills will allow you to improve your presentation in your other Key Skills.

- If you feel comfortable and confident with the assessment, don't forget to keep on practising and developing your IT skills. You may also want to talk to your tutors about Level 4 IT.

Planning and selecting information (page 18)

1. Yahoo, Hotbot, Lycos, Altavista, Infoseek… to name but a few.

2. Examples of two sites are www.consumerisminternational.org and www.gmworld.newscientist.com

3. The Guardian had many articles on GM foods for example:

   GM Foods Split Labour   February 15, 1999

   GM Foods, Questions and Answers   June 2, 1999

4.

From:	Mark Jones<MS@Jones.freeserve.co.uk>
To:	JonSmith@smithy.freeserve.co.uk>
Sent:	22 May 2000 11:39
Subject:	GM Foods – Project

Hi Smithy

Below are 2 great sites for our project which I found browsing the net.

www.consumerisminternational.org

and

www.gmworld.newscientist.com

Mark

Developing information (page 21)

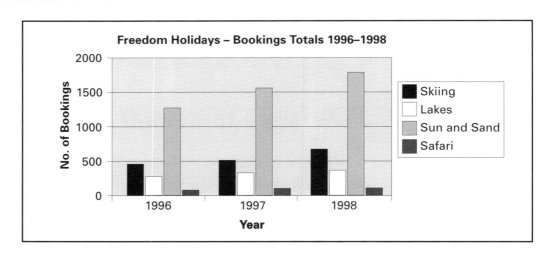

Presenting information (page 23)

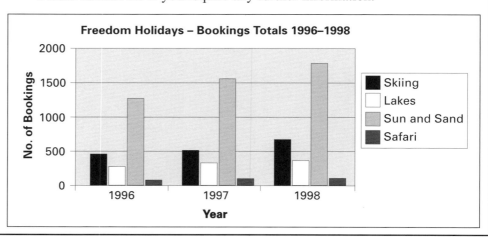

Task 1

RSPCA Shop Account Jan - Feb 00

ITEM	Purchased	Wholesale Price	Sold	Retail Price
Pencils	200	£0.03	100	£0.06
Plastic Wallets	1000	£0.10	357	£0.15
Biros Blue	1000	£0.08	86	£0.25
Biros Black	1000	£0.08	58	£0.25
Rubbers	1000	£0.04	45	£0.15
Wallet Folders	250	£0.15	113	£0.30
Correction fluid	60	£0.42	37	£0.65
Labels	30	£0.56	30	£0.74
TOTALS	4540		826	

RSPCA Shop Account Jan - Feb 00

ITEM	Purchased	Wholesale Price	Wholesale Expenditure	Sold	Retail Price	Retail Income
Pencils	200	£0.03	£6.00	100	£0.06	£6.00
Plastic Wallets	1000	£0.10	£100.00	357	£0.15	£53.55
Biros Blue	1000	£0.08	£80.00	86	£0.25	£21.50
Biros Black	1000	£0.08	£80.00	58	£0.25	£14.50
Rubbers	1000	£0.04	£40.00	45	£0.15	£6.75
Wallet Folders	250	£0.15	£37.50	113	£0.30	£33.90
Correction fluid	60	£0.42	£25.20	37	£0.65	£24.05
Labels	30	£0.56	£16.80	30	£0.74	£22.20
TOTALS	4540		£385.50	826		£182.45

RSPCA Shop Account Jan - Feb 00

ITEM	Purchased	Wholesale Price	Wholesale Expenditure	Sold	Retail Price	Retail Income
Pencils	200	0.03	=B4*C4	100	0.06	=E4*F4
Plastic Wallets	1000	0.1	=B5*C5	357	0.15	=E5*F5
Biros Blue	1000	0.08	=B6*C6	86	0.25	=E6*F6
Biros Black	1000	0.08	=B7*C7	58	0.25	=E7*F7
Rubbers	1000	0.04	=B8*C8	45	0.15	=E8*F8
Wallet Folders	250	0.15	=B9*C9	113	0.30	=E9*F9
Correction fluid	60	0.42	=B10*C10	37	0.65	=E10*F10
Labels	30	0.56	=B11*C11	30	0.74	=E11*F11
TOTALS	=SUM(B4:B11)		=SUM(D4:D11)	=SUM(E4:E11)		=SUM(G4:G11)

Task 2

RSPCA Shop Account Jan - Feb 00

ITEM	Purchased	Wholesale Price	Wholesale Expenditure	Sold	Retail Price	Retail Income	EVALUATION
Pencils	200	£0.03	£6.00	100	£0.06	£6.00	STOCK
Plastic Wallets	1000	£0.10	£100.00	357	£0.15	£53.55	CANCEL
Biros Blue	1000	£0.08	£80.00	86	£0.25	£21.50	CANCEL
Biros Black	1000	£0.08	£80.00	58	£0.25	£14.50	CANCEL
Rubbers	1000	£0.04	£40.00	45	£0.15	£6.75	CANCEL
Wallet Folders	250	£0.15	£37.50	113	£0.30	£33.90	CANCEL
Correction fluid	60	£0.42	£25.20	37	£0.65	£24.05	STOCK
Labels	30	£0.56	£16.80	30	£0.74	£22.20	STOCK
TOTALS	4540		£385.50	826		£182.45	

RSPCA Shop Account Jan - Feb 00

ITEM	Purchased	Wholesale Price	Wholesale Expenditure	Sold	Retail Price	Retail Income	EVALUATION
Pencils	200	0.03	=B4*C4	100	0.06	=E4*F4	=IF(E4/B4<50%,"CANCEL","STOCK")
Plastic Wallets	1000	0.1	=B5*C5	357	0.15	=E5*F5	=IF(E5/B5<50%,"CANCEL","STOCK")
Biros Blue	1000	0.08	=B6*C6	86	0.25	=E6*F6	=IF(E6/B6<50%,"CANCEL","STOCK")
Biros Black	1000	0.08	=B7*C7	58	0.25	=E7*F7	=IF(E7/B7<50%,"CANCEL","STOCK")
Rubbers	1000	0.04	=B8*C8	45	0.15	=E8*F8	=IF(E8/B9<50%,"CANCEL","STOCK")
Wallet Folders	250	0.15	=B9*C9	113	0.30	=E9*F9	=IF(E9/B9<50%,"CANCEL","STOCK")
Correction fluid	60	0.42	=B10*C10	37	0.65	=E10*F10	=IF(E10/B10<50%,"CANCEL","STOCK")
Labels	30	0.56	=B11*C11	30	0.74	=E11*F11	=IF(E11/B11<50%,"CANCEL","STOCK")
TOTALS	=SUM(B4:B11)		=SUM(D4:D11)	=SUM(E4:E11)		=SUM(G4:G11)	

Task 3

RSPCA SHOP ACCOUNTS

The accounts for the period January - February this year show that, although sales of some items continue to do well, some do not seem so popular.

I have calculated those items where we still have only sold half of our stock. I propose that we discontinue these items.

I think we should conduct a questionnaire among other students to see what they would like the shop to stock.

ITEM	Purchased	Wholesale Price	Wholesale Expenditure	Sold	Retail Price	Retail Income	EVALUATION
Pencils	200	£0.03	£6.00	100	£0.06	£6.00	STOCK
Plastic Wallets	1000	£0.10	£100.00	357	£0.15	£53.55	CANCEL
Biros Blue	1000	£0.08	£80.00	86	£0.25	£21.50	CANCEL
Biros Black	1000	£0.08	£80.00	58	£0.25	£14.50	CANCEL
Rubbers	1000	£0.04	£40.00	45	£0.15	£6.75	CANCEL
Wallet Folders	250	£0.15	£37.50	113	£0.30	£33.90	CANCEL
Correction fluid	60	£0.42	£25.20	37	£0.65	£24.05	STOCK
Labels	30	£0.56	£16.80	30	£0.74	£22.20	STOCK
TOTALS	4540		£385.50	826		£182.45	

Exemplar Test – model answer

Task 1

Sue Dent – Video Dbase1   16/09/00

③ All fields have appropriate titles and data types. (4 marks)

② Title (2 marks)

Certificate	Video Title	Running Time	Price
12	King Ralph	102	£1.00
15	The Piano	90	£2.00
18	The Shining	120	£1.50
15	Ghost	110	£2.00
15	Back Beat	124	£2.00
18	The Exorcist	105	£1.00
15	My Life	100	£1.00
12	Bird on a Wire	140	£1.00
PG	Free Willy	120	£2.00
PG	Hocus Pocus	95	£1.50
18	Carrie	126	£1.00
PG	Mrs Doubtfire	150	£1.50
15	Sniper	107	£1.00

① A database has been created in Microsoft Access. (2 marks)

④ Enter data. (6 marks)
Check the accuracy of your keying in. (1 mark)

⑤ This printout must be handed in as part of your evidence for your E.A.I. Check for accuracy. (1 mark)

Page 1

Sue Dent – Video Dbase1   16/09/00

The field headings have been centred and highlighted for effect.

Certificate	Video Title	Running Time	Price
		0	£0.00
12	Bird on a Wire	140	£1.00
12	King Ralph	102	£1.00
15	Patch Adams	105	£2.00
15	The Haunting	105	£2.00
15	Urban Legend	105	£2.00
15	Sniper	107	£1.00
15	The Piano	90	£2.00
15	My Life	100	£1.00
15	Back Beat	124	£2.00
15	Ghost	110	£2.00
18	Carrie	126	£1.00
18	The Shining	120	£1.50
18	The Exorcist	105	£2.00
PG	Hocus Pocus	95	£1.50
PG	Mrs Doubtfire	150	£1.50
PG	Free Willy	120	£2.00

⑥ 3 videos have been added. (2 marks)

Make sure you print out gridlines.

⑦ Records are sorted by ascending order. (2 marks)

⑧ Check for accuracy. Save. Print. (1 mark)

Page 1

Task 2

Query 1 ←   16/09/00

Task 2
Perform a query
① Videos less than £2.
With a certificate 12.
(4 marks)

Sorted against 'criteria'. →

Certificate	Video Title	Running Time	Price
12	Bird on a Wire	140	£1.00
12	King Ralph	102	£1.00

Page 1

Sue Dent – Certificate 12   16/09/00

③ Add name and 'Cert 12'.
(2 marks)

Certificate	Video Title	Price
King Ralph	12	£1.00
Bird on a Wire	12	£1.00

② Columns rearranged
with video titles first
and running time
deleted. (4 marks)

④ Check for accuracy.
Save.
Print. (2 marks)

Page 1

Task 3

① Using a DTP program, such as PUBLISHER – Statement of sale.
Bold.
Large. (3 marks)

VIDEO SALE

Phone 020 8123 4567
for further details

Example of WORDART

Don't miss this 'one off' opportunity to snap up a bargain.

For full details of titles see Page 2

Vary font and size

② Suitable image and resize. (3 marks)

④ Footer and page number. (3 marks)

Sue Dent-Leaflet,1

Task 3 continued

③ List of videos imported from database.
Not including price. (4 marks)

Certificate	Video Title	Running Time
12	Bird on a Wire	140
12	King Ralph	102
15	Patch Adams	105
15	The Haunting	105
15	Urban Legend	105
15	Sniper	107
15	The Piano	90
15	My Life	100
15	Back Beat	124
15	Ghost	110
18	Carrie	126
18	The Shining	120
18	The Exorcist	105
PG	Hocus Pocus	95
PG	Mrs Doubtfire	150
PG	Free Willy	120

⑤ Check leaflet for accuracy.
Save with suitable file name.
Print. (3 marks)

④ Footer and page
number. (3 marks)

Sue Dent-Leaflet,2

Video Sale Leaflet.pub

Video Shop.mdb

⑥ Print out your files. (1 mark)

Appendices

A Information Technology Level 3 – Unit Specification

B Action Plans – including a completed version

C Witness Testimonies – including a completed version

D Proxy Qualifications

E Where to find out more

F Glossary

KEY SKILLS UNIT

Information technology

What is this unit about?

This unit is about applying your IT skills to suit different purposes.

You will show you can:

- plan and use different sources to search for and select information;

- explore, develop and exchange information, and derive new information;

- present information, including text, numbers and images.

How do I use the information in this unit?

There are three parts to this unit: what you need to know, what you must do and guidance.

Part **A**
WHAT YOU NEED TO KNOW

This part of the unit tells you what you need to learn and practise to feel confident about applying IT skills in your studies, work or other aspects of your life.

Part **B**
WHAT YOU MUST DO

This part of the unit describes the skills you must show. All your work for this section will be assessed. You must have evidence that you can do all the things listed in the bullet points.

Part **C**
GUIDANCE

This part describes some activities you might like to use to develop and show your IT skills. It also contains examples of the sort of evidence you could produce to prove you have the skills required.

LEVEL 3

Part A

WHAT YOU NEED TO KNOW

In planning and selecting information,

YOU NEED TO KNOW HOW TO:

- plan a substantial activity by breaking it down into a series of tasks;

- compare the advantages and limitations of different sources of information *(eg databases, the internet, material to be scanned, files on disk, CD-ROMs)* and select those suitable for your purpose *(eg to obtain views of others, to produce financial data, product information or a multi-media presentation)*;

- choose appropriate techniques for finding information *(eg database query techniques, internet search engines, multiple criteria including relational operators such as less than/greater than, and logical criteria such as AND/OR/NOT conditions)* and use them to carry out effective searches;

- make selections based on relevance to your purpose and judgements on quality *(eg your own and others' views on accuracy and reliability of content)*.

In developing information,

YOU NEED TO KNOW HOW TO:

- enter and bring together information in a consistent form *(eg lists, tables, frames, types of images)* and use automated routines *(eg macros, icons, database query and report routines, validation for database entries)*;

- create and use structures and procedures for developing text, images and numbers *(eg sort and group information, use mail-merge, analyse and interpret numerical data using spreadsheet software, generate graphs and charts)*;

- explore information *(eg design and develop lines of enquiry, change values and rules in a model to make predictions and test hypotheses)*;

- derive new information *(eg evaluate information from different sources to reach and justify a conclusion, use facilities to calculate or deduce results)*;

- use methods of exchanging information to support your purpose *(eg e-mail, shared access to documents, collaborative development of information)*.

In presenting information,

YOU NEED TO KNOW HOW TO:

- develop the structure of your presentation *(eg modify templates and paragraph styles, apply automatic referencing facilities such as page numbers, dates and file names)*, and use the views of others to guide refinements *(eg obtain feedback on content, layout, format, style)*;

- develop and refine the presentation of text, images and numbers *(eg improve impact by changing format or layout, combine information, overlay images on text)*;

- present information so that it meets your purpose and the needs of the audience *(eg compare paper based, single form, mixed form and multi-media presentations and choose the most suitable one available)*;

- ensure work is accurate and makes sense *(eg proof-read, use a spell-checker, seek the views of others)*.

You will also need to know: the implications of using IT, comparing your use of IT with systems used elsewhere; when it is necessary to observe copyright or confidentiality; how to save your work for easy retrieval, for managing versions and to avoid loss; how to identify errors and their causes and minimise risks from viruses; and how to work safely and minimise health risks.

Part B

WHAT YOU MUST DO

You must:

Plan and carry through at least one substantial activity that includes tasks for IT3.1, IT3.2 and IT3.3.

Evidence must show you can:

IT3.1

Plan and use different sources to search for, and select, information required for **two** different purposes.

- plan how to obtain and use the information required to meet the purpose of your activity;
- choose appropriate sources and techniques for finding information and carry out effective searches; and
- make selections based on judgements of relevance and quality.

IT3.2

Explore, develop and exchange information, and derive new information, to meet **two** different purposes.

- enter and bring together information in a consistent form, using automated routines where appropriate;
- create and use appropriate structures and procedures to explore and develop information and derive new information; and
- use effective methods of exchanging information to support your purpose.

IT3.3

Present information from different sources for **two** different purposes and audiences.

Your work must include at least **one** example of text, **one** example of images and **one** example of numbers.

- develop the structure and content of your presentation using the views of others, where appropriate, to guide refinements;
- present information effectively, using a format and style that suits your purpose and audience; and
- ensure your work is accurate and makes sense.

Part C

GUIDANCE

Examples of activities you might use

You will have opportunities to develop and apply your IT skills during your work, studies or other activities. For example, when:

- planning, carrying out and reporting findings from an investigation or project;
- designing and presenting a product;
- researching information and reporting outcomes to customers or clients;
- exchanging information and ideas with work colleagues or other students.

You will need time to practise your skills and prepare for assessment. So it is important to plan ahead. For example, to identify an activity that is substantial enough to provide opportunities for following through tasks for IT3.1, IT3.2 and IT3.3. You may need to do additional tasks to cover all the requirements of Part B.

The purpose for using IT can be decided by you or by other people, but you must make sure that the work you produce suits this purpose. Using IT can contribute evidence of your use of other key skills, such as communication and application of number.

This unit is for use in programmes starting from September 2000.

QCA/99/342   First published 1999 ISBN 1 85838 402 8

Copyright © 1999 Qualifications and Curriculum Authority.

Reproduction, storage, adaption or translation, in any form or by any means, of this publication is prohibited without prior written permission of the publisher, or within the terms of licences issued by the Copyright Licensing Agency. Excerpts may be reproduced for the purpose of research, private study, criticism or review, or by educational institutions solely for educational purposes, without permission, providing full acknowledgement is given.

Printed in Great Britain.

The Qualifications and Curriculum Authority is an exempt charity under Schedule 2 of the Charities Act 1993.

Qualifications and Curriculum Authority,
29 Bolton Street, London W1Y 7PD.
www.qca.org.uk   Chairman: Sir William Stubbs.

Copies of this document may be obtained using the QCA *Publications List and Order Form* or by contacting:
QCA Publications, PO Box 99, Sudbury, Suffolk, CO10 6SN.
Telephone: 01787 884444, Fax: 01787 312950.
When ordering, please quote title and reference number.

You will need to think about the quality of your IT skills and check your evidence covers all the requirements in Part B.

Examples of evidence

3.1 PLAN, AND SELECT INFORMATION

A description of the substantial activity and tasks. A plan for obtaining and using the information required.

Print-outs of the relevant information with notes of sources compared and used. Notes on how you made searches and selected information.

3.2 DEVELOP INFORMATION

Print-outs, with notes, or a record from an assessor who observed your use of IT, showing how you have exchanged, explored and developed information and derived new information.

Notes of automated routines.

3.3 PRESENT INFORMATION

Working drafts, or a record from an assessor who observed your screen displays, showing how you developed the presentation using information from different sources.

Print-outs or a static or dynamic screen display of your final work, including examples of text, images and numbers.

If producing certain types of evidence creates difficulties, through disability or for another reason, you may be able to use other ways to show your achievement. Ask your tutor or supervisor for further information.

Key Skills Action Plan

NAME:

DATE:

KEY SKILL:

LEVEL:

DATE	Planned Tasks	Review Date	Completed Date	Evidence Component	Check links with other Key Skills

Student Signature

Tutor Signature

Date

Key Skills Action Plan

NAME: Angela Thomas

DATE: 7 September 2000

KEY SKILL: IT

LEVEL: 3

DATE	Planned Tasks	Review Date	Completed Date	Evidence Component	Check links with other Key Skills
10/9	Speak to Mrs Edwards about my project	14/9	11/9	3.1	LP 3.1
14/9	Internet search for information on Psychology degree courses	16/9	15/9	3.1	C 3.2
	Email universities for further information				
20/9	Produce rough draft of booklet on Psychology degree course. Probably using WORD and PUBLISHER	25/9	24/9	3.2	C 3.2
25/9	Tutorial with Mrs Edwards		25/9	3.2	LP 3.2
26/9	Design questionnaire for my Psychology tutor group	5/11	3/11	3.2	C 3.3 N 3.1
1/11– 6/11	Can't use IT drop-in room as closed for upgrading				
6/11	Work on my presentation for Psychology tutor group for December 6	24/11	6/12	3.2, 3.3	C 3.1b
13/11	Wordprocess report for Mrs Edwards	6/12	12/12	3.2. 3.3	LP 3.2, 3.3
20/11	Tutorial		20/11	3.3	LP 3.2, 3.3

Student Signature   *A Thomas*   Tutor Signature   *CEdwards*   Date   14/12/2000

N.B. Action Plans are not required as evidence for Key Skill IT, but they are a really good way for students to keep a track of the work they are doing and make **LINKS** with other **Key Skills**

WITNESS TESTIMONY

Student Name: Key Skill:

EVIDENCE COMPONENT OBSERVED:

DESCRIPTION OF ACTIVITY:
DATE ACTIVITY TOOK PLACE:
CONTEXT:

How did the candidate meet the requirements of the Unit Specification?

Continue overleaf if necessary.

WITNESS SIGNATURE:
WITNESS STATUS:

Contact Address
Tel:
DATE:

Student Signature
Date:

WITNESS TESTIMONY

Student Name: Angela Thomas   **Key Skill:** Information Technology

EVIDENCE COMPONENT OBSERVED: IT 3.1

DESCRIPTION OF ACTIVITY: Library search
DATE ACTIVITY TOOK PLACE: 14 September 2000
CONTEXT: Angela has chosen to investigate Psychology degree courses at a range of universities. She intends to produce her results as an advice booklet for other students and as a presentation for her Psychlogy A/S Level tutor group.

How did the candidate meet the requirements of the Unit Specification?

Angela had shown me her plan for her IT portfolio and had produced an Action Plan to help guide her through the Evidence Components.

On 14 September 2000, I observed Angela in the school library using the Internet to obtain information about Psychology degree courses. She used both the ALTA VISTA and LYCOS search engines. She was able to refine her SEARCH CRITERIA when her initial research was unproductive.

Angela visited the UCAS site and downloaded pages from the site. She later printed them out and identified the universities that she would investigate further.

Over the course of her session in the library, Angela obtained information from 30 university sites.

I questioned Angela on her knowledge of the Internet and her answers are attached.

Continue overleaf if necessary.

WITNESS SIGNATURE: Chris Edwards
WITNESS STATUS: ICT Tutor

Contact Address Newtown College, Newtown
Tel: 01566 879923
DATE: 24/11/2000

Student Signature *A Thomas*
Date: *27/11/2000*

D Proxy Qualifications

Details of proxy qualifications to act as exemptions from parts of the Key Skills Qualification. Parts A and B apply.

Part A (External Assessment)

English Language or Literature, Gaelic and Welsh, and Communication

Mathematics[1] and Application of Number

GCE AS/A Level A-E examination performance provides exemption for the external test in these Key Skills at Level 3.

GCSE A*-C examination performance provides exemption for the external test in these Key Skills at Level 2.

GCSE D-G examination performance provides exemption for the external test in these Key Skills at Level 1.

Computing[1] or ICT[1] and Information Technology

GCE A Level A-E performance provides full exemption for the Key Skill at Level 3.

GCE AS A-E performance provides exemption for the external test in the Key Skill at Level 3.

GCSE A*-C performance provides full exemption for the Key Skill at Level 2.

GCSE D-G performance provides full exemption for the Key Skill at Level 1.

GCSE Short Course ICT[1] and Information Technology

A*-C performance provides exemption for the external test in the Key Skill at Level 2 and also for one of the two specified purposes of the internal Key Skill component at Level 2.

D-G performance provides exemption for the external test in the Key Skill at Level 1 and also for one of the two specified purposes of the internal Key Skill component at Level 1.

Part Award, Single Award or Double Award in Vocational A Level and GNVQ or Part One GNVQ in ICT[1] and Information Technology

Vocational AS/A Level (Advanced GNVQ) A-E performance provides full exemption for the Key Skill at Level 3.

Intermediate GNVQ or Part One GNVQ Pass/Merit/Distinction performance provides full exemption for the Key Skill at Level 2.

Foundation GNVQ or Part One GNVQ Pass/Merit/Distinction performance provides full exemption for the Key Skill at Level 1.

The currency of qualification specifications

The above exemptions have been confirmed for those specifications accredited by the regulatory authorities. Revision to accredited specifications would result in the exemptions offered by that subject being reviewed and if necessary revised or removed.

The currency of examination performance

The currency of exemptions provided by proxy qualifications must be no longer than three years from the date of award to the date of claim. In these circumstances, exemptions from September 2000 can only be claimed for qualifications gained after September 1997.

[1] This applies to all qualifications whether gained through the medium of English, Gaelic or Welsh

Part B (Portfolio)

NATIONAL QUALIFICATIONS FRAMEWORK

The following titles for English, Mathematics and ICT Qualifications provide exemptions to the external assessment of the Key Skills.

For the Communication Key Skill

ENGLISH

GCSE English

GCSE English Literature

GCE AS and Advanced English Language

GCE AS and Advanced English Language and Literature

For the Application of Number Key Skill

MATHEMATICS

GCSE Mathematics

GCE AS or GCE Advanced Mathematics

GCE AS or GCE Advanced Pure Mathematics

GCE AS or GCE Advanced Further Mathematics

GCE AS or GCE Advanced Statistics

GCE AS Mechanics

GCE AS Discrete Mathematics

GCE AS Applied Mathematics

For the IT Key Skill

ICT

GCSE IT

GCSE (Short Course) ICT

GCE AS ICT

GCE AS Computing

GCE A ICT

GCE A Computing

GNVQ Foundation ICT (6-unit award)

GNVQ Foundation ICT (3-unit award)

GNVQ Intermediate ICT (6-unit award)

GNVQ Intermediate ICT (3-unit award

GNVQ Advanced ICT (12-unit award)

GNVQ Advanced ICT (6-unit award)

GNVQ Advanced ICT (3-unit award)

Useful websites

Association of Colleges (AoC)
www.aoc.co.uk

BBC Further Education
www.bbc.co.uk/education/fe
www.bbc.co.uk/education/fe/skills/index.shtml

Department for Education and Employment
www.dfee.gov.uk
If you are involved in producing a Progress File you can gain help from
www.dfee.gov.uk/progfile/index.htm

Further Education Development Agency (FEDA) – the main body leading Key
Skills developments in schools and colleges.
www.feda.ac.uk

For **GNVQ support** try
www.feda.ac.uk/gnvq

National Extension College (NEC) – produces useful material to support Key
Skills development.
www.nec.ac.uk/index.html

Qualifications and Curriculum Authority (QCA) – the organisation
responsible for the development, implementation and quality assurance of all national
qualifications.
www.qca.org.uk

University and Colleges Admissions Service (UCAS)
www.ucas.ac.uk

Letts Educational
www.letts-education.com

Application — An item of software designed to carry out a specific task e.g. word processing or accounting

Automated routine — Procedures, such as macros or database queries

Automatic referencing — Page numbers, dates and file names that will appear on each page of your document

Auto sum — The button on the menu that allows you to add up automatically a column in a spreadsheet

Backup — A copy of your file made for security purposes

CD-ROM — A method of storing and retrieving electronic information from a CD. Compact Disk - Read Only Memory.

Cell — The basic element in a spreadsheet. Can contain text, numbers, formulae or references to other cells.

Clip art — Images stored in files that can be imported into other files, often found in desktop publishing packages

Column — The information going from top to bottom of a page: this page has three columns

Copyright — This identifies the person(s) responsible for creating the work. It is theft to take their work or ideas.

CPU or Tower — Central Processing Unit – the box of the computer

Database — An application used for storing, sorting and reporting on data. Structured into fields and records.

Disk drive — Originally used to describe floppy disk drives and given letters, A, B etc. A hard disk is also a disk drive and is usually given the letter C. They are where you store data – either software or the files you create.

Edit — To change the way a file or document looks, e.g. inserting, deleting, spell-checking

Email — Electronic mail sent via a modem, computer to computer

File — A document or data stored on a disk

Font — The complete set of characters belonging to a typeface

Footer — Information printed automatically at the bottom of a page, can contain the filename, date, time etc.

Format — Formatting a document changes the way it looks, e.g. justification, paragraphing etc.

Formula — A mathematical function that allows you to perform the same calculation on a range of cells, usually in a spreadsheet

Graphs — A visual display of data plotted against X and Y axes

Hard copy — A printout of your file

Hardware — The computer, printer, scanner etc.

Header — Information printed automatically on the top of a page that can contain filename, date, time etc.

HTML — Hypertext mark up language, the language used for writing web pages

Hypothesis — A suggested explanation for a group of data or facts, awaiting further verification

Icon — A small picture that can be used to select an instruction to your computer

Image — A visual representation of data, e.g. graphs, charts, clip art etc.

Import — To bring data from one file into another, e.g. putting a clip art picture into a Word document

Internet — An international network of computers that can be joined by anyone with a computer, a telephone line and a modem. Information is shared through email and the world wide web.

Justification — Changing the way the sides or edges of a document look, either straight or ragged. Full justification means both edges are blocked in straight lines.

Keyboard — The most common way to enter data into a computer

Load — To transfer information from storage to the computer system

Macros — Using them allows you to automatically produce a series of keystrokes so that one keystroke can take the place of many, e.g. putting your name and address at the top of a letter

Mailmerge — Allows you to create form letters, mailing labels and envelopes. You can organise the address data and merge it into a generic document.

Margins — The space at the sides and top and bottom of a document that will be free from print

Monitor — The screen or visual display unit (VDU)

Mouse — An external device that can be used to select options or portions of text

Multimedia — Software combining text and graphs with motion and sound, using video, audio and photographs

Multi-page — A combined document that includes pagination, number, text and images consisting of 4 pages or more

Numbers — Many software applications allow you to demonstrate that you can perform mathematical and statistical calculations

Package — An alternative name for an application or program

Page break — A division between one page and another that can be inserted automatically by the application or done by the user

Pagination — A feature that breaks up text into prescribed amounts to fit on a page; numbering can be added by the user

Row — The cells going horizontally in a spreadsheet or table

Save — The storing of a file on disk

Search and replace — Allows the automatic search for a word, phrase or character to be replaced by another

Software — Name for all types of computer programs

Spell-check — A facility in the application that checks for spelling errors. Does not check for synonyms.

Text — The words that you type into a document/file

Virus — A series of commands that can attach themselves to and destroy the information in your files